ATTITUDES
AT EVERY
ALTITUDE

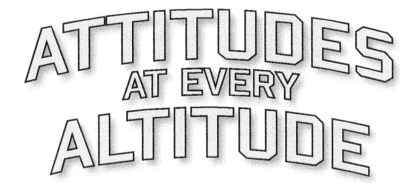

ATTITUDES AT EVERY ALTITUDE

GREGG PROTEAUX

Beaver's Pond Press, Inc.

Edina, Minnesota

ISBN 10: 1-59298-266-2
ISBN 13: 978-1-59298-266-0

Library of Congress Control Number: 2008939955
Printed in the United States of America
First Printing: January 2009
13   12   11   10   09   6   5   4   3   2   1

Cover and interior design by Clay Schotzko

Beaver's Pond Press, Inc.

Beaver's Pond Press is an imprint of
Beaver's Pond Group
7104 Ohms Lane
Edina, MN 55439-2129
(952) 829-8818
www.BeaversPondPress.com

To order, visit www.BookHouseFulfillment.com
or call (800) 901-3480. Reseller discounts available.

DEDICATION

This writing is dedicated to my two children, Garrett and Chloe' who have survived having not just one parent as a flight attendant but both mother and father.

Thank you for all of your love and support. May God bless you and be with you always.

Love, Dad

ACKNOWLEDGMENTS

Assembling this list of friends has brought back some great memories for me during the years of this wonderful career. I am grateful that all of you are still a part of my life and that you have been so generous. My warmest thanks and appreciation to all of you . . .

Ann, Beverly, Carol, Colleen, David, Donn, Elaine, Elizabeth, Ellen, Glen, Janette, Jean, Jennifer, Jilane, Jim, Jo, Joanna, Joanne, Kathy, Kristine, Marcy, Margaret, Martina, MaryRose, Nancy, Rene, Roxanne, Ruth, Sheri, Susan, Tara, Terry, Theresa, Tim, Tracy, and Veronica.

WELCOME PASSENGERS

On behalf of this airline and this flight crew (and isn't that how they all start), we would like to welcome you aboard a few actual situations that occur on airplanes almost every day.
YOU are probably in this book !

Have you ever told a flight attendant how many ice cubes to put into your glass? YOU are in here!

Have you ever asked a flight attendant, "Where are we?" YOU are in here!

That is all okay; a lot of people have never flown before. Were a lot of people never taught consideration for others? Were a lot of people never taught patience?

Perhaps YOU are not in here!

Oh well, travel through these pages and you will probably find your family and friends in here somewhere!

WELCOME ABOARD!

PROLOGUE

Do you remember when your parents saw that advertisement in the newspaper that the local airline was going to have a Flight Attendant Open House on January 17, nineteen hundred and something, at a nearby airport hotel? Well, perhaps by now you think that your mother should have gone instead of her sending you!

THE OPEN HOUSE—You entered a huge hotel ballroom set theater style for 100. Remember a recruiter gave you a flight attendant job description and an airline timetable? The front of the room consisted of three chairs off to the left and a speaker's podium to the right. By now you were really wondering, what is this all about? Within five minutes every seat was occupied and no one spoke a word to anyone. All of the "candidates" were dressed the same (well, at least those that had a clue) in their navy blue or black suits. Some were wearing jeans, had not combed their hair in six months, and appeared that they had just stopped by on their way to the beach! The recruiters gave you a pretty clear description of the position (at least you thought it was pretty clear at the time) and what to expect in training and during that probationary period. They told you something about "seniority" and "reserve" but by then you didn't have a clue about what all of that really meant, you just wanted the job! By now, you didn't even care if they paid you. You just wanted the travel privileges, the layovers, the uniform and the wings. You heard something about union membership and just thought, "sign me up!" right?

Well, now each "candidate" was given approximately two minutes to stand up and introduce himself to the group (and didn't some of them say some stupid things; "my mother thought I should come here today," "I love to fly and I would like to take my camera around the world," and now only 98 more to go!) While each "candidate" was introducing himself, those three recruiters up there were writing as fast as they could. By the time number 45 stood up, you were thinking that this is really messed up and you need to get out of there; but you stayed! Well, that session ended and the recruiters thanked you for coming and if they could offer you "further encouragement" they would be in touch with you within 10 days. What did that mean? What is "further encouragement?"

THE INTERVIEW—Well, you did or said something that the recruiters liked in that Open House of 100 last week that got you a one-on-one interview at the airline's world headquarters. (Can you believe that your father drove you to the interview so that you would not get lost and so that you would be on time!) You were dressed in the same navy blue suit that you wore to the Open House and you thought that you were ready for your interview. The recruiter went through a series of about one dozen questions with you . . . by the way, in the interview did you ever tell them any of the following?

— That you never planned to work after 5 p.m. on Fridays and never work longer than two day trips!

— That you don't clean up throw up!

— That you don't do "head counts!"

— That you would not go through with the beverage cart more than once during a 3 1/2 hour flight!

— That you never planned to get your hair all back to one color!

— That you do not own a wristwatch with a second hand!

— That you still planned to wear two ankle bracelets and three graduated length chains!

Well, since you did not tell them all of the things that you were not going to do, the airline gave you the job!

THE JOB—The physical, the drug screening test, the background investigation, oh, no! Six weeks of unpaid training, three to four tests per week, training flights on weekends and no sleep. You really wonder now, what have I gotten myself into? Graduation luncheon, the last meal that the airline will entertain you with until your 25th anniversary. Remember in the interview when they asked you "are you willing to relocate" and you thought "yes" to the local airport, 11 miles away. Not quite! One-third of your class would be based in New York City, one-third in Chicago and one-third in Los Angeles. Now you get an idea of what "seniority" really means! You are #37 in your class of 40 and you are assigned to Los Angeles, 1, 379 miles from what you called home. You almost quit but your parents think this will be good for you as they have their pass privileges all planned out for the next five years!

There you are in Los Angeles, sharing a two-bedroom apartment with five other flight attendants, on "reserve" waiting for the phone to ring. You can't even take a part-time job because you only have 10 scheduled days off per month and scheduling always seems to alter the days off. You thought that "reserve" would last four or five months but instead it was 4 1/2 years! Messed up? By now, Los Angeles is called home and you are somewhat intrigued with the other airline that is locally based in Los Angeles. You went to their Open

House only to find that all new hires would be based in either Miami or New York City. You would drop $7.37 per hour, go back on "reserve" and your new "seniority" number would be 12,749. Forget it!

Well, that was several years ago and today you are at the same carrier that you interviewed with on January 17th. Not much has changed, has it? After all of these years, a few changes:

— Your check-in time has been changed to 15 minutes earlier for domestic flights.

— The flight attendant parking lot is now three miles farther away from the airport while the pilots park on the airport property.

— The crew bus has not been washed in three years.

— The check-in person is having a bad day almost every day now.

— You are still short meals three legs out of four.

— Management still requests that you "write up things." However, you don't see any changes after all of these years of "write ups."

— Tray tables are in worse shape than ever and have not been cleaned since the aircraft went into service nine years ago.

But, none of this matters:

— Your favorite part of the job?—the time off!

— The ability to drop trips—great!

— What would you miss most if you quit?—the friends!

— The travel privileges—lunch in Little Rock this week and dinner in Dayton next week!

— The lifestyle is wonderful and the variety is like no other.

— There is never any work to take home.

— No computers, no telephones and you do not come back from lunch and return 17 messages.

Isn't this one of the nicest careers around? You are finally grateful that your mother sent you to that Open House on January 17th. Sure, there are a few schedule changes, a few delays, some duplicate seating challenges, your paycheck may seldom be correct, a few too many carry-on bags, a few hot meals, some new surcharges and a lot of passengers that think that just because they bought a round-trip ticket, they now own the airline. What would you rather do? If you have any idea of leaving to "explore other interests," please do it soon as many of us would really like to move up one more seniority number! Meanwhile, sit back, relax, and enjoy the in-flight service.

JUST WHAT EVERY FLIGHT ATTENDANT NEEDS . . .

One more passenger asking if he can have another cocktail while the flight attendants are in the midst of doing the safety demonstration.

Right, the drinks are complimentary in first class and the passengers will certainly get their share. But can't they be content with one on the ground and the next seventeen while in the air?

ONE MORE EXCUSE FOR A FLIGHT ATTENDANT'S BAD ATTITUDE IS . . .

Knowing that you, as a new hire, will be "on reserve" for at least the next six years.

Reserve indicates "on call." A flight attendant could be called at 4 a.m. for a 6 a.m. departure. Who wants to live this way for the next six to 16 years plus work every weekend? A lot of flight attendants do.

PAYING PASSENGERS
REALLY DON'T WANT . . .

137 hot meals for 160 passengers

Catering is never responsible. So, wouldn't one expect those flight attendants to count every meal in those ovens along with checking emergency equipment, lavatory fire extinguishers, ice, juice, pop, cups, counting the paper towels, garbage bags, napkins and getting those pilots a beverage? All before passengers begin boarding?

FLIGHT ATTENDANTS
DON'T NEED . . .

A migraine headache, on a three-day trip, without their medication.

A flight attendant is 700 miles from the closest pharmacy and has accumulated over 300 hours of sick time. The airline has put the fear of God in them about ever using any of those hours. It makes many flight attendants even sicker at the thought of calling in sick!

THE LAST THING A FLIGHT ATTENDANT WANTS IS A LATE CHECK-IN AT THE AIRPORT AND . . .

A passenger thinking he is going to Birmingham although the plane is bound for Billings.

Nineteen announcements in the gate area indicating that an aircraft is going to Billings probably means it is going to Billings! Once passengers enter the terminal, they should start reading the signs and listening to the announcements. Forget about whether the babysitters will pick up the kids after school; stop wondering if they have turned off the heat and unplugged the coffee pots; don't worry about finding the cars when they return. If passengers miss their planes, they will have a lot more than babysitting problems to worry about.

ALL THAT A FLIGHT ATTENDANT NEEDS IS ANOTHER CUT IN PAY AND . . .

A 250-pound beverage cart with a brake that does not work.

Those carts have brakes like automobiles; sometimes they don't hold. Does anyone have any idea of how many back injuries and back surgeries take place on flight attendants each year because of those carts?

JUST WHAT EVERY FLIGHT ATTENDANT NEEDS . . .

A four-hour flight delay that scheduling did not tell you about!

Exactly why is it that communication is so difficult in this industry? Many scheduling departments are not even in the same state where flight attendants originate their flights. As a matter of fact, most flight attendants wouldn't know a scheduler if they saw one. I wonder why schedulers don't introduce themselves when they fly.

ONE MORE EXCUSE FOR A FLIGHT ATTENDANT'S BAD ATTITUDE IS . . .

That the FAA gets on the aircraft and your company-issued flashlight is at home.

Although there are about eight flashlights already located on most aircraft, every flight attendant is required to carry his/her own. There really are some pretty strange rules around here.

PAYING PASSENGERS REALLY DON'T WANT . . .

To be required to lift their own ninety-pound, fifty-five-inch carry-on bag into that bin that only accommodates a forty-six inch bag!

It is not the passenger's fault. "Someone" should have told them that the overhead bins have weight and size restrictions. It is not the passenger's fault!

FLIGHT ATTENDANTS
DON'T NEED . . .

A passenger that has been drinking for the past seven months.

Ticket agents, please don't tell us one more time that the drunk passenger will be fine once he gets up into the air. You just said that you were going to call the airport police to have him removed from the gate area, but then he settled down. If you think that he will be fine, why don't you get on and ride with him?

THE LAST THING A FLIGHT
ATTENDANT WANTS IS A
LATE CHECK-IN AT
THE AIRPORT AND . . .

A burnt meal to be served to the cockpit crew.

Flight attendants don't burn meals intentionally. Pilots are responsible for a lot. We give them the best we have to offer. Heaven knows that they probably get enough burnt meals at home!

ALL THAT A FLIGHT ATTENDANT NEEDS IS ANOTHER CUT IN PAY AND . . .

A full-uniform appearance at the downtown bar.

Flight attendants don't drink in uniform in public. Do they really stay out too late? Do flight attendants drink?

JUST WHAT EVERY FLIGHT ATTENDANT NEEDS . . .

Another passenger asking if there is a vegetarian option for the meal.

The answer is "no vegetarian option," so the passenger settles for a beverage . . . until the flight attendant gets three rows past and then the passenger requests the meal. Are they suddenly no longer a vegetarian? I really don't get it!

ONE MORE EXCUSE FOR A FLIGHT ATTENDANT'S BAD ATTITUDE IS . . .

Realizing that the plane is one hour away from landing in Honolulu and that there are no "Plants and Animals Declaration" forms on board.

This form is to be completed by each passenger entering the state of Hawaii. Where are all of these thousands of forms filed each day? Would the passengers have to turn around and go back home if they ever ran out of these forms?

FLIGHT ATTENDANTS DON'T NEED . . .

One more passenger who has figured out how to open the compartment containing the oxygen masks.

Do you think that the flight attendants should be able to explain every wire, tube and screw in there? Both the passengers and the airlines expect way too much of us!

PAYING PASSENGERS
REALLY DON'T WANT . . .

To have flight attendants moving their rolling bags and thirty-five Jamaican walking sticks that they claim are blocking the emergency life raft.

For some reason the FAA and the airline do not consider rolling bags and walking sticks as emergency equipment, to be placed into the bin that is placarded "emergency equipment only." Many flight attendants working today have flown in excess of forty years and really know and follow the regulations. Just don't mess with them! Thirty-five walking sticks?

THE LAST THING A FLIGHT
ATTENDANT WANTS IS A LATE
CHECK-IN AT THE AIRPORT AND . . .

To learn that this aircraft is number twenty-seven in line for take off at New York's JFK airport.

Do you know that number twenty-seven in line can sometimes mean a forty- to fifty-minute wait prior to takeoff? Is this just another "industry standard"?

ALL THAT A FLIGHT ATTENDANT NEEDS IS ANOTHER CUT IN PAY AND . . .

A 6:00 a.m. showing–three days running–for a 5:45 a.m. check-in time.

Aflight attendant is considered late when checked in at 6:00 a.m. although their pay does not begin until departure time at 6:45 a.m. Who else shows up for work one hour before the time clock starts? Isn't this "industry standard" messed up?

JUST WHAT EVERY FLIGHT ATTENDANT NEEDS . . .

Catering has boarded 265 hot meals without silverware.

Just a hint: Passengers should bring their own utensils with them. Flight attendants do. As a matter of fact, flight attendants are probably carrying peanut butter, crackers, tuna, soup, salad, yogurt—just about everything that the local supermarket carries. Many passengers do, too.

ONE MORE EXCUSE FOR A FLIGHT ATTENDANT'S BAD ATTITUDE IS . . .

A random drug testing that his/her urine sample is below ninety degrees.

A drug test is not valid if the urine is below ninety degrees. Way too many drug screenings today and it is very expensive for these airlines. Flight attendants wear rubber gloves to pick up garbage, but why do those drug screeners?

PAYING PASSENGERS REALLY DON'T WANT . . .

Their antique musical instrument to reappear in eighty-nine pieces after the flight attendants have tried to accommodate it on the lower galley elevator.

Flight attendants, the elevator is for crew members, beverage carts, and meal carts only! It is not meant for guitars, cellos, or pianos. No wonder so many musicians travel by bus.

FLIGHT ATTENDANTS DON'T NEED . . .

Three random drug screenings in one month.

I n safety-sensitive positions such as these, pilots and flight attendants are given occasional drug screenings to be certain that they are not using illegal drugs, while the airline is feeding crew members poppy seed muffins as part of the crew meals. Are these drug screenings really random? Really?

JUST WHAT EVERY FLIGHT ATTENDANT NEEDS . . .

To remember that they are not getting paid for today's five-hour delay.

F light attendants get paid only while the engines are running. They can be on duty for nine hours and twenty minutes, get paid for six hours, and call it normal. Would you even think of going to work at 7 a.m. knowing that your pay will not start until noon?

THE LAST THING A FLIGHT ATTENDANT WANTS IS A LATE CHECK-IN AT THE AIRPORT AND . . .

Their crocheting project left behind on their jumpseat.

The airline policy is no crocheting, knitting, rug hooking or crossword puzzles on the jumpseats, even though service has been completed and 2 ½ hours remain in flight. The company wants flight attendants in the aisle every ten to twelve minutes talking to the passengers and pouring more coffee. Is it really the frequency of "aisle checks" or is it the price of the ticket and the time schedule that will bring the passengers back? Don't let the flight attendants ever sit down!

ALL THAT A FLIGHT ATTENDANT NEEDS IS ANOTHER CUT IN PAY AND . . .

A six-week wait before turning in their liquor deposit.

The liquor deposit is simply the cash collected from sales during a flight. Flight attendants are probably using that money for six weeks. After all, when they are first hired they are only bringing home about $311 per week. The liquor deposit is just a small loan until the food stamps start coming in.

ONE MORE EXCUSE FOR A FLIGHT ATTENDANT'S BAD ATTITUDE IS . . .

Forgetting to move his/her clock forward one hour in the spring.

When it is 9 a.m. in Las Vegas, some flight attendants know the correct time in Tokyo. However, they cannot get the time correct at home in April. Any late check-ins that day?

FLIGHT ATTENDANTS DON'T NEED . . .

Another passenger on a seven-hour flight who is just amazed that flight attendants get to eat too!

If I were at home, I probably would have had two or three meals by now. Don't people that work in offices eat most every day? Will flight attendants ever be viewed as normal people?

~~~

THE LAST THING A FLIGHT ATTENDANT WANTS IS A LATE CHECK-IN AT THE AIRPORT AND . . .

Another flight attendant on their schedule for the entire month whose attitude is worse than theirs.

And it really is embarrassing when all of the flight attendants are in a bad mood on the same flight. Come on! A lot of us only fly ten days each month; we can do this.

ALL THAT A FLIGHT ATTENDANT NEEDS IS ANOTHER CUT IN PAY AND . . .

The idea that in the "chain of command," you, as Lead Flight Attendant, come before the captain.

Today, many flight attendants are older than the pilots (and the planes), but the pilots really are in charge. Just ask them.

JUST WHAT EVERY FLIGHT ATTENDANT NEEDS . . .

The Lead Flight Attendant is now older than Santa Claus's mother.

Have you noticed that there has not been much turnover in this career in recent years? This is the career that no one quits. How old is Santa Claus's mother?

ONE MORE EXCUSE FOR A FLIGHT ATTENDANT'S BAD ATTITUDE IS . . .

Seventy-seven passengers claiming that their ear phones do not work when the movie is almost over.

Hey flight attendants, start believing the passengers and give them their money back. If you do not give them the refund, the airline may accidently show a profit for the quarter.

FLIGHT ATTENDANTS DON'T NEED . . .

A passenger trying to do the safety demonstration with them.

At least someone is paying attention. It seems as though sixty-five percent of the passengers are sleeping through this very important part of the flight attendant's job. Next time, please discontinue the conversation with the person next to you, put down the newspaper and pretend you are paying attention.

THE LAST THING A FLIGHT ATTENDANT WANTS IS A LATE CHECK-IN AT THE AIRPORT AND . . .

A reminder to insert last year's revisions into their company-issued flight attendant manual.

F light attendants are not always the best at record-keeping. Just ask the Federal Aviation Administration. Does anyone know that this manual consists of about 70,000 pages covering job details? That is just the job description!

ALL THAT A FLIGHT ATTENDANT NEEDS IS ANOTHER CUT IN PAY AND . . .

A passenger's hand coming around the closed galley curtain holding a napkin, tissue and a dirty coffee cup.

I f flight attendants would go through the aisle every ten or twelve minutes, as directed by the airline, passengers would not have to bring their trash into the galley. Flight attendants, take turns and spend more time in the aisle!

JUST WHAT EVERY FLIGHT ATTENDANT NEEDS . . .

The passenger that wants to change her baby's diaper on the galley counter.

This is a mess. When was the last time anyone changed their infant's diapers on the center island in their kitchen? Perhaps one of the lavatories has a changing table. Keep those babies out of the galleys!

ONE MORE EXCUSE FOR A FLIGHT ATTENDANT'S BAD ATTITUDE IS . . .

A passenger coming on board with his own twelve-pack of beer.

It appears that the passenger has already consumed twenty-four cans before bringing on his own twelve-pack. Passengers, don't even think of bringing your own beer onto an airplane. It is against all regulations, at all airlines, to open your own beer. Now you know!

PAYING PASSENGERS
REALLY DON'T WANT . . .

A flight attendant telling them that they did not pay the other flight attendant for the drink they just consumed!

This occurs way too often! Oh well, flight attendants have larger issues than this, much larger!

FLIGHT ATTENDANTS
DON'T NEED . . .

Another passenger asking over and over, "Where are we now?"

Guess what? Flight attendants don't usually have a clue. When we are traveling from New York to Miami, I just tell them that we are twenty miles north of Salt Lake City and when we are traveling from Dallas to Los Angeles, I tell them that we are twenty miles north of Atlanta.

THE LAST THING A FLIGHT ATTENDANT WANTS IS A LATE CHECK-IN AT THE AIRPORT AND . . .

A pilot who has lost his way.

Don't worry too much about this; it's unheard of. Oh yes, occasionally an aircraft may land at the wrong airport. Don't worry too much about that either.

FLIGHT ATTENDANTS DON'T NEED . . .

Passengers asking, worriedly, "Did you just put on a parachute?" after the flight attendants have strapped into their jumpseats.

Never mind the way it looks. It really is just a seat belt with shoulder straps. Airlines think a lot of their flight attendants, but a parachute?

ALL THAT A FLIGHT ATTENDANT NEEDS IS ANOTHER CUT IN PAY AND . . .

To find oneself in need of a tetanus shot because of the horrific slash on one's arm from trying to get that 250-pound beverage cart out of its stowage compartment.

When the wheels on those carts turn sideways, most everyone throws their back out at least once. Oh, in addition to the tetanus shot, one mustn't forget the flu shot. The airline just hates it when one uses their sick time. Isn't it after calling in sick three times over a twelve-month period that one must report to a manager's office?

JUST WHAT EVERY FLIGHT ATTENDANT NEEDS . . .

The passenger seated in the emergency exit row who thinks he knows more about the operation of the door than the flight attendant.

Flight attendants really hope that he has not ever seen the operation of that door as we don't ever want to witness it ourselves. Aren't passengers curious though?

ONE MORE EXCUSE FOR A FLIGHT ATTENDANT'S BAD ATTITUDE IS . . .

The discovery that every seat has been occupied on every "leg" for the past thirty days.

A "leg" is a flight from one city to another. It's very nice to have a few vacant seats occasionally. Passengers have some space to move around and the flight attendants see a reduction in complaints. It's interesting that every seat is occupied on every "leg" for the past thirty days and the airline continues to show a loss!

ALL THAT A FLIGHT ATTENDANT NEEDS IS ANOTHER CUT IN PAY AND . . .

A passenger asking if you will assist him in lifting his 350-pound carry-on bag into the overhead bin.

The flight attendant's answer will always be "no." Please check the bag at the ticket counter as the overhead bins have a maximum weight limit (unlike today's flight attendants).

THE LAST THING A FLIGHT ATTENDANT WANTS IS A LATE CHECK-IN AT THE AIRPORT AND . . .

Seventeen passengers waiting to use the lavatory before the seat belt sign has even been turned off.

These lavatories are small, dirty and smelly. Try using the restroom in the airport terminal before boarding the aircraft. They are much larger and cleaned every hour.

JUST WHAT EVERY FLIGHT ATTENDANT NEEDS . . .

Six unruly passengers on board without any "violation notice" forms on board.

One never wants to see a "violation notice," as this often indicates that the police will be meeting the passenger upon arrival at their destination. Sit back, relax and enjoy the next three-hour flight because the flight attendants are in charge and the passengers are not. Why is it so difficult for some to give up that control? Give it up and relax!

ONE MORE EXCUSE FOR A FLIGHT ATTENDANT'S BAD ATTITUDE IS . . .

To hear one more time, "I will have mine medium rare!"

If a passenger brought his own meal with him, it may be medium rare. But when was the last time one was served anything on an airplane that required a knife?

FLIGHT ATTENDANTS DON'T NEED . . .

To be asked out for dinner by a pilot and then the pilot expects the flight attendant to pay.

Do pilots really like having the reputation of being cheap? Pilots don't pay for newspapers. Within three minutes of the last passenger getting off the airplane, pilots are going through seat pockets looking for newspapers left on board by the passengers. Those dailies must be up to fifty cents now.

THE LAST THING A FLIGHT ATTENDANT WANTS IS A LATE CHECK-IN AT THE AIRPORT AND . . .

Three passengers boarding in aisle chairs headed for the emergency exit row.

The aisle chair is the narrow wheelchair that fits down the aisle, and passengers seated in exit rows are expected to assist other passengers in the event of an evacuation. Does anyone think that these passengers want to assist others out of the aircraft and down the wing to safety? Ticket agents, please be more careful who is assigned to the exit row.

ALL THAT A FLIGHT ATTENDANT NEEDS IS ANOTHER CUT IN PAY AND . . .

Due to back injuries, the flight attendant has more stitches in their back than in their uniform blazer!

Yes, as the health insurance benefits decrease, let's increase the weight of those beverage carts by another 100 pounds. I suppose that it is just another "industry standard."

JUST WHAT EVERY FLIGHT ATTENDANT NEEDS . . .

Passengers asking the flight attendants if this flight bound for Honolulu is going through Memphis because there is an Elvis look-alike on board.

Is it because the airline boarding music is an Elvis song or is it that some of the crew members appear to look like Elvis? You know, many of those pilots can sing!

ONE MORE EXCUSE FOR A FLIGHT ATTENDANT'S BAD ATTITUDE IS . . .

Another three-day trip without a galley curtain.

This just means a whole lot more passenger contact. Can you believe that many flight attendants are shy, quiet and withdrawn, and don't like travel or public contact? Someone has made some big mistakes in the hiring process, haven't they!

FLIGHT ATTENDANTS DON'T NEED . . .

Three complaint letters in their file within one week.

Do you know that passengers write letters to the airline when a flight attendant forgets to bring them a tissue, another cup of coffee, a glass of water, or even when the flight attendant throws a bag of chips at them? Please give the flight attendants a break; after all, many of them work ten or eleven days every month!

THE LAST THING A FLIGHT ATTENDANT WANTS IS A LATE CHECK-IN AT THE AIRPORT AND . . .

Their co-workers' makeup bags weighing more than their clothes bags for the five-day trip.

One could make a good living by selling cosmetics just to flight attendants. Could a few flight attendants cut down on the perfume before we receive one more passenger complaint letter indicating that the flight attendants wear too much! These airplanes sure can get small.

ALL THAT A FLIGHT ATTENDANT NEEDS IS ANOTHER CUT IN PAY AND . . .

150 passengers and 150 overcooked meals.

Would this be the proper time to remind the passengers that the meal is complimentary? Well, it was complimentary ten years ago! Today, the pretzels and chips don't ever see an oven. Thank your lucky stars!

JUST WHAT EVERY FLIGHT ATTENDANT NEEDS . . .

The highlight of their day: to clean another airplane lavatory.

Not to say that airplane lavatories aren't clean! It is best if one can be the first to use it before boarding starts at 5:30 a.m. After 5:30 a.m. just don't go in there!

~~~~~

ONE MORE EXCUSE FOR A FLIGHT ATTENDANT'S BAD ATTITUDE IS . . .

Another flight from Dallas to Las Vegas with well over a hundred cowboy hats.

Just take an airplane ride during the Las Vegas rodeo. Because of all of those cowboy hats hanging over into the aisle, the aisle narrows from eighteen inches wide to four inches.

PAYING PASSENGERS REALLY
DON'T NEED . . .

One more flight attendant telling them that they will have to wait approximately 10 minutes before they can have a pillow.

This occurs frequently. The flight attendants will be in the aisle in approximately 10 minutes "selling" travel pack pillows for passengers to take with them. Airlines, don't raise the airfare a nickel to cover expenses, just have the flight attendants trying to sell pillows, blankets, head sets, chips and corn dogs! Cotton candy is on its way! Wait 10 minutes!

FLIGHT ATTENDANTS
DON'T NEED . . .

A cart partner with bulemia.

Seriously, some flight attendants need to get to a gym and acquire some muscle mass. Encourage your flight attendants to eat on those 18-hour flights!

THE LAST THING A FLIGHT ATTENDANT WANTS IS A LATE CHECK-IN AT THE AIRPORT AND . . .

When preparing to come up from the lower galley, the flight attendant realizes that neither the passenger lift nor the cart lift is operating.

When the lifts or elevators are not operating, the flight attendants must climb up a ladder and fit through an 18-inch by 22-inch hole in the main floor of the aircraft. But then there's the 259 meals. Don't worry about the fact that flight attendants aren't going to get 259 meals through that hole, but who could fit through a hole measuring 18-by-22-inches? A flight attendant!

ALL THAT A FLIGHT ATTENDANT NEEDS IS ANOTHER CUT IN PAY AND . . .

154 passengers returning from Cancun with only one working lavatory on the aircraft.

Was it the meal on the aircraft a week ago, the meal on the cruise ship, or the burrito in Cancun? Oh well, only one lavatory is operational! Then again, we could opt for a two-day delay to get it repaired in Cancun.

JUST WHAT EVERY FLIGHT ATTENDANT NEEDS . . .

One more passenger handing garbage to the flight attendants while they are still serving meals.

How would you feel about being the next person served after a flight attendant has picked up the garbage from the previous person? The flight attendants will be coming through with a separate garbage cart later. This really is a dirty job!

ONE MORE EXCUSE FOR A FLIGHT ATTENDANT'S BAD ATTITUDE IS . . .

The realization–while in the custom's line– that . . . their passport expired last year.

The airline will probably remove the flight attendant from payroll for the next 60 to 90 days. The passport is just another required item along with the wristwatch, manual, wings, FAA identification, and flashlight. Hey flight attendants, check your passport expiration date today!

FLIGHT ATTENDANTS DON'T NEED . . .

A full flight headed to Detroit only to find that not even one can of Vernors Ginger Ale is on board.

Lighten the load, save the fuel, and get the ginger ale off the aircraft! Two tablespoons of coke into a glass of 7-Up will make ginger ale! Try it, you may just like it!

THE LAST THING A FLIGHT ATTENDANT WANTS IS A LATE CHECK-IN AT THE AIRPORT AND . . .

Three other oversized flight attendants stuck in a lower galley elevator built to accommodate only one flight attendant.

S tuck flight attendants make the workload too heavy on the other six flight attendants already serving passengers. Either one flight attendant or one cart but certainly not three flight attendants of today's proportions!

JUST WHAT EVERY FLIGHT ATTENDANT NEEDS . . .

A pilot who cannot tell his left from his right!

T his is a minor concern. Consider the idea that many pilots can no longer hear.

ALL THAT A FLIGHT ATTENDANT NEEDS IS ANOTHER CUT IN PAY AND . . .

One more article with a headline reading, "Airlines Report Lower Passenger Traffic in July."

And there has not been one vacant seat on one flight in the past 49 days! Are the airlines not satisfied unless they have overbooked and turned away 14 passengers from every flight? If airlines did not overbook on some flights, they would never be full—but to overbook every flight? How much is 14 passengers times 72 flights per day times $200 per passenger? Oh, flight attendants, please watch the number of napkins that you use!

ONE MORE EXCUSE FOR A FLIGHT ATTENDANT'S BAD ATTITUDE IS . . .

The flight attendant's jumpseat falls to the floor when their cart partner sits down next to them.

For 45 years the airlines had a requirement of height and weight in proportion. And for good reason. Are those jumpseats really just attached to the wall with velcro?

~~~~~

FLIGHT ATTENDANTS DON'T NEED . . .

When the announcement is made during a medical emergency for an "RN" to step forward, three "Red Necks" come forward.

We sincerely appreciate it when all of the medically trained professionals step forward when this announcement is made. "Red Necks," just remain seated and we will bring you another beer!

THE LAST THING A FLIGHT ATTENDANT WANTS IS A LATE CHECK-IN AT THE AIRPORT AND . . .

Six unaccompanied minors who have discovered the flight-attendant call button before take-off.

U naccompanied minors are those under the age of 15 years traveling without a parent. Does a flight attendant really replace the parent for the four-hour flight? Parents, some flight attendants can't take care of a plant!

ALL THAT A FLIGHT ATTENDANT NEEDS IS ANOTHER CUT IN PAY AND . . .

The realization that the seat in the emergency exit row is being occupied by a gentleman who is older than water.

The emergency exit rows are to be occupied by the ABPs. Able-Bodied Persons are expected to assist in an emergency evacuation—lift the 45 pound exit door, toss it out of the aircraft, crawl out onto the wing, etc., etc. How old is water anyway?

ONE MORE EXCUSE FOR A FLIGHT ATTENDANT'S BAD ATTITUDE IS . . .

Two flight attendant hiring mistakes on the same beverage cart.

Can you believe that some airlines will receive as many as 100 applications per day for the flight attendant position, interview 600, and hire only 70? Sometimes airlines will hire flight attendants that have no business being in a customer contact position. Oh, have you seen a few?

JUST WHAT EVERY FLIGHT ATTENDANT NEEDS ...

To question themselves on their car ride home, "Did I disarm my door?"

If the aircraft door is not "disarmed," the slide will blow out and inflate the next time that anyone opens that door. This negligence could cost the airline about $25,000 to repack the slide and could result in the death of the individual opening the door. "Cross check, cross check and cross check." Now, don't you really think that they expect too much of us? This job demands perfection, don't you think?

THE LAST THING A FLIGHT ATTENDANT WANTS IS A LATE CHECK-IN AT THE AIRPORT AND ...

Two flat tires on the aircraft in the same day!

Flat tires on an aircraft can take hours to replace, depending on where the aircraft is. Guess what! No pay for the seven-hour delay. No pay! This is an "industry standard"!

FLIGHT ATTENDANTS DON'T NEED . . .

To have another flight attendant bid their next month's schedule for them.

A fellow flight attendant bids the next month's flight schedule for you and you end up on four, six-day trips, flying over every weekend. Your sister is getting married on the first Saturday of the month, you have not worked weekends for years, no one will trade with you, and the company can't help you. Suddenly, that 23 year seniority isn't worth much, is it? Isn't seniority all that flight attendants have?

ALL THAT A FLIGHT ATTENDANT NEEDS IS ANOTHER CUT IN PAY AND . . .

The cost of their cosmetics consistently exceeding $100 every week.

This phenomenon occurs when the flight attendant is only bringing home $403 per week. Why is it that when the flight attendant is bringing home $900 per week, she's wearing less makeup? Shouldn't it be the opposite?

JUST WHAT EVERY FLIGHT ATTENDANT NEEDS . . .

The passengers seated in A, B and C of the emergency exit row were just released from the Mayo Clinic three hours ago!

Would one really feel comfortable assisting 147 passengers during an evacuation of an aircraft after having spent the past three months in any medical facility? There are requirements for passengers seated in those emergency exit rows. What are they?

~~~~~

ONE MORE EXCUSE FOR A FLIGHT ATTENDANT'S BAD ATTITUDE IS . . .

Another passenger asking, "Is this lavatory for men or women?"

Okay, here is the policy: Use whichever lavatory becomes vacant first, one person at a time. Do you know that only about 50% of passengers actually flush? Look for the little flat button that usually reads, "flush" or "push," normally located on the back wall of the toilet or on the wall closest to the sink.

PAYING PASSENGERS
REALLY DON'T WANT . . .

Another flight attendant refusing to hold their crate during the flight.

The crate measures three feet by four feet. The flight attendants really don't have any secret stowage compartments. Just check the crate next time. Oh, it's fragile? Then ship it with lots of packing material.

FLIGHT ATTENDANTS
DON'T NEED . . .

To have an FAA inspector on board the aircraft when seven out of eight flight attendants are in the lower galley at the same time.

The FAA never wants more than two flight attendants down there at the same time. Is it really for safety reasons, or is it just in case a passenger needs a Band-Aid™, tissue, aspirin, oxygen or defibrillator? Perhaps a passenger just wants another cup of tea! Nothing is too much for our customers!

THE LAST THING A FLIGHT ATTENDANT WANTS IS A LATE CHECK-IN AND . . .

One more passenger with plugged ears, thinking he is speaking in a normal volume, when he's actually screaming.

Everyone's ears plug at times, but screaming usually awakens many passengers nearby. Flight attendants really don't think you're yelling at them, but you are scaring the other passengers.

ALL THAT A FLIGHT ATTENDANT NEEDS IS ANOTHER CUT IN PAY AND . . .

One more passenger handing over a dirty diaper saying, "Here, take this!"

The passenger seated behind you, about to receive his meal, would not like the flight attendant to be handling the dirty diaper as his appetizer. Hint: Dispose of diapers in the lavatory trash disposal located next to the sink. Any lavatory on board is acceptable.

JUST WHAT EVERY FLIGHT ATTENDANT NEEDS . . .

A battery-powered exit light as a Christmas present from your flight attendant manager.

D id your flight attendant manager remove an exit sign from an aircraft to give to you as a Christmas present? Oh, but flight attendant, don't ever walk off the aircraft with a napkin; THAT belongs to the airline.

ONE MORE EXCUSE FOR A FLIGHT ATTENDANT'S BAD ATTITUDE IS . . .

Three kindergarten children who have been assigned the emergency exit row.

T he minimum age to sit there is fifteen. Even you, as the parent, cannot sit in the emergency exit row as long as you have children under fifteen seated in another row on the same airplane. "Someone" thinks that you would be more concerned about your children than assisting in an evacuation. The airlines have a lot of rules. Right?

FLIGHT ATTENDANTS DON'T NEED . . .

To be working with another flight attendant who has not smiled at a passenger in 17 years.

Flight attendants, smile! If the passengers do not like the flight attendants, they may not fly this airline again, and when the passengers do not come back no one will have a job. Enough airlines have gone out of business in the past few years. A few smiles could even avoid a few face lifts, too!

~~~~~~~

THE LAST THING A FLIGHT ATTENDANT WANTS IS A LATE CHECK-IN AT THE AIRPORT AND . . .

10 oxygen panels dropping during take-off!

Some of these airplanes are only one year old and only cost about $47 million each. However, a few of those oxygen panels located above your head tend to be a little loose. It's okay; the mechanics know how to repack those things!

ALL THAT A FLIGHT ATTENDANT NEEDS IS ANOTHER CUT IN PAY AND . . .

The discovery that the last 49 passengers in the lavatory have pushed their used hand towels into the tissue dispenser and not into the trash disposal.

N ow, this is a mess! Please, place dirty hand towels in the dispenser marked "Trash." One hundred towels on the floor are really awful!

FLIGHT ATTENDANTS DON'T NEED . . .

One more passenger in row 17 telling them that he's allergic to the cat assigned to row 15.

T his is really a mess! What is the difference between a small computer bag under the seat and a small carry-on pet kennel under the seat? The difference is about $65 one way! Isn't almost everyone allergic to cats? How could an airline accommodate them both? Without a few vacant seats, they can't.

JUST WHAT EVERY FLIGHT ATTENDANT NEEDS . . .

Two overweight pilots who could never fit through those flight deck windows!

Perhaps too much sitting! Why don't they get out of the cockpit, into the aisle, push a cart and smile at 700 passengers some day? I guess we all have choices, don't we? or . . .

ONE MORE EXCUSE FOR A FLIGHT ATTENDANT'S BAD ATTITUDE IS . . .

One more passenger asking, "Where are we?"

Always feel free to ask. The flight attendants don't usually know or care as they are so busy serving meals, getting oxygen for the passenger in 7-D, or getting aspirin for 24-A. Flight attendants will ask the pilots to make an announcement once the pilots have figured out where they are!

THE LAST THING A FLIGHT ATTENDANT WANTS IS A LATE CHECK-IN AT THE AIRPORT AND . . .

Passengers asking, "Don't you have Coors beer?"

S uggestion to the president of the airline: Remove all beer from the airplane forever. Passengers having to settle for something other than their beer of choice isn't a pretty sight. Remove the beer!

ALL THAT A FLIGHT ATTENDANT NEEDS IS ANOTHER CUT IN PAY AND . . .

A 102-year-old passenger traveling alone whose 82-year-old son said, "She will be just fine!"

C ould the 82-year-old son just come along with the 102-year-old mother? She usually requires oxygen within the first-half hour of the flight, if she even lives through the duration of the 55-minute flight.

JUST WHAT EVERY FLIGHT ATTENDANT NEEDS . . .

Another passenger asking if he can have your wings!

Yes, here is a set of plastic wings that the airline provides. However, if the passenger would like some pretty gold wings, they will need to attend six weeks of Flight Attendant Training which includes about nine hours of classroom per day, about 16 written tests (on which one needs to score ninety percent or higher), and at least two training flights. During the training period, the airline will pay you about $37 per day. Still interested?

ONE MORE EXCUSE FOR A FLIGHT ATTENDANT'S BAD ATTITUDE IS . . .

The discovery of an apple or orange in their bag as they head through the customs area.

R emember, no fresh fruits or vegetables through customs for anyone. Some flight attendants travel with enough food for a five-day trip even though they will be gone for only twelve hours. Well, take a look at some of them! (Is overeating the reason, or is it the airline food?)

PAYING PASSENGERS REALLY DON'T WANT . . .

To have to ask the flight attendant if they can borrow the flight attendant's flashlight because their reading light does not work.

J ust move the passenger. Oh, that's right, there has not been a vacant seat for the past three months. Why is the airline reporting a loss for this quarter?

FLIGHT ATTENDANTS DON'T NEED . . .

The passenger in row one asking, just as the entry door is being closed, "How do you know that everyone is on board?"

The secret is that the gate agent told the flight attendants that everyone is accounted for. Another secret is that, for the most part, flight attendants don't care if everyone is on board or not! A few vacant seats would be wonderful!

THE LAST THING A FLIGHT ATTENDANT WANTS IS A LATE CHECK-IN AT THE AIRPORT AND . . .

Another passenger ordering the number of ice cubes to put into their glass!

Hint: Tell the flight attendant how many ice cubes you want before the beverage is poured. Did you know that liquid is easier to digest without ice?

ALL THAT A FLIGHT ATTENDANT NEEDS IS ANOTHER CUT IN PAY AND . . .

The owner of the airline seated in 1-C.

Does anyone really think that flight attendants are going to perform their jobs any differently because he/she is there? The job is what it is. The airplane is only as clean as it is. Gate agents get concerned, but the owner doesn't usually want special attention. So, let's all relax and enjoy the flight.

JUST WHAT EVERY FLIGHT ATTENDANT NEEDS . . .

A passenger asking if he can walk through the airplane to collect the pop tops for his group's fundraiser!

Good idea! Will you kindly pick up a few tissues, water bottles, dirty diapers, and air sick bags along the way? Passengers can be so helpful at times!

ONE MORE EXCUSE FOR A FLIGHT ATTENDANT'S BAD ATTITUDE IS . . .

Your cart partner's belief that closing the galley curtain will make the galley soundproof.

Don't you hate hearing every word those flight attendants are saying behind that curtain . . . or even in front of it! Now that the curtains are mesh, they aren't very soundproof any more. Were they ever?

FLIGHT ATTENDANTS DON'T NEED . . .

Another passenger opening the closet door thinking that it is the lavatory!

This actually happens almost every day. Unseasoned passengers believe that the closet is the lavatory until they see the 16 hangers. This closet is not for crew luggage, shoes, car seats, musical instruments, antiques, toilet paper or soap, but rather for the valuable garments of first-class passengers. Coach passengers, don't even ask!

THE LAST THING A FLIGHT ATTENDANT WANTS IS A LATE CHECK-IN AT THE AIRPORT AND . . .

Having heated the meals, discovering that the previous crew left two plastic cup trays on the lower rack in the oven.

Can you picture those plastic cup trays after they had been in a 400-degree oven for 20 minutes? Hopefully no fire extinguisher was required!

ALL THAT A FLIGHT ATTENDANT NEEDS IS ANOTHER CUT IN PAY AND . . .

The 12-year-old passenger who wants to open the oxygen panel to see how it works.

His parents, seated next to him, think this is okay. This is million-dollar equipment. Flight attendants aren't even allowed to play with this stuff.

JUST WHAT EVERY FLIGHT ATTENDANT NEEDS . . .

One more passenger asking, "Why can't I just leave my tray table down for landing?"

In an emergency, it would be too difficult for passengers to maneuver around tray tables. Flight attendants are trained to get the aircraft evacuated in about 90 seconds. No flight attendant is going to wait around in a smoke-filled cabin while a passenger is playing with that tray table. Get it?

ONE MORE EXCUSE FOR A FLIGHT ATTENDANT'S BAD ATTITUDE IS . . .

A cart partner who consistently forgets to put coffee into the coffee-maker filter tray.

Are you ready? No filter in the tray, no coffee in the pot. There are a couple of choices here: either serve a lot of tea or bid to work with someone different next month.

FLIGHT ATTENDANTS DON'T NEED ...

One more passenger telling them, upon exiting the lavatory, that the blue water won't stop flushing.

Toilets on airplanes use about a million gallons of water per flush while the ones at home only use about one gallon. It really is okay. Just one more reason why the airlines are in financial distress.

THE LAST THING A FLIGHT ATTENDANT WANTS IS A LATE CHECK-IN AT THE AIRPORT AND ...

A passenger on a 52-minute flight asking, "What movie are we going to see?"

It is unfortunate that we don't have a projector, no screen, no sound, and no movie. Just a 52-minute flight! How about a free beverage and some free chips? Oh, never mind. The free treats are a thing of the past.

ALL THAT A FLIGHT ATTENDANT NEEDS IS ANOTHER CUT IN PAY AND . . .

The passenger who complains that his coffee cup was not filled to the brim just as the seat belt sign has come on and the aircraft is about to drop 85 feet!

Flight attendants really do try to be reasonable about turbulence. Passengers should feel free to ask for a refill of coffee once the seat belt sign has been turned off. That is, if they can find a flight attendant.

JUST WHAT EVERY FLIGHT ATTENDANT NEEDS . . .

Another passenger asking, "Where do you go when you are on vacation?"

Many flight attendants really hope that they can stay within ten miles of their house. Once asked, "Do flight attendants live in houses?" a flight attendant replied, "No, we live in tents. The airline busses us down to the airport from tent farms in the northern part of the state."

ONE MORE EXCUSE FOR A FLIGHT ATTENDANT'S BAD ATTITUDE IS . . .

A full midnight flight of sleeping passengers and the only reading light that doesn't work is located above the only passenger that would like to read.

149 occupied seats and one passenger that would like to read. Flight attendants, start carrying an extra flashlight with you. That solution is a lot easier than answering to management later as to why you didn't move the passenger to another seat. You hate to remind management that the flight did not have any vacant seats.

FLIGHT ATTENDANTS DON'T NEED . . .

An overweight passenger saying that his tray table is broken because it only falls six inches down from the seatback!

That is okay. The two-ticketed passengers can enjoy their two meals without the tray tables.

THE LAST THING A FLIGHT ATTENDANT WANTS IS A LATE CHECK-IN AT THE AIRPORT AND . . .

A passenger who has consumed two vodkas and three beers asking if he can go sit in the cockpit.

There are two hours and thirty-five minutes left in the flight. Have another sandwich and take a nap!

ALL THAT A FLIGHT ATTENDANT NEEDS IS ANOTHER CUT IN PAY AND . . .

One more passenger asking if flight attendants are ever scared!

If a flight attendant ever tells a passenger that he or she is not scared, the flight attendant is telling the passenger a little white lie. Would a flight attendant ever lie to a passenger?

JUST WHAT EVERY FLIGHT ATTENDANT NEEDS . . .

While boarding in Las Vegas in August, the temperature is 114 degrees, the window shades have been closed to keep the aircraft cooler, and a passenger says, "Oh, the other airplane that we flew on had windows."

Do you think she's kidding? That's okay, not everyone flies every day.

ONE MORE EXCUSE FOR A FLIGHT ATTENDANT'S BAD ADDTIUDE IS . . .

The forward jumpseat that has not retracted for the past five days.

The FAA wants that jumpseat to retract against the wall or passengers might have to step over it on the way out the door. The FAA can be so picky. Can't they?

FLIGHT ATTENDANTS DON'T NEED . . .

The passenger on the aircraft trying to adjust the light fixture above thinking that it's an air vent!

Hint: The air vents move, but the reading lights do not!

THE LAST THING A FLIGHT ATTENDANT WANTS IS A LATE CHECK-IN AT THE AIRPORT AND . . .

The flight attendant who takes up more than half of the double jumpseat.

Picture this: Each flight attendant has about thirteen inches of space while the passenger's assigned seat is about eighteen inches wide. Whatever happened to height and weight in proportion for those flight attendants?

ALL THAT A FLIGHT ATTENDANT NEEDS IS ANOTHER CUT IN PAY AND . . .

Passengers who feel the pillow is for them to take home for their infant's crib and that the blanket would make a good throw for the home.

When was that pillow last cleaned? Does anyone really think the blanket is a good match for their couch? Well, that was last year. Now passengers can pay for them and legally take them home.

JUST WHAT EVERY FLIGHT ATTENDANT NEEDS . . .

The female passenger asking the female flight attendant, "What is the number on the bottle of the hair color that you use?"

Which color? The flight attendant has five different colors in her hair. Between flights, attendants certainly have time to play with their hair and it doesn't always look good for the effort. Passengers will ask anything though, won't they?

ONE MORE EXCUSE FOR A FLIGHT ATTENDANT'S BAD ATTITUDE IS. . .

The deplaning passenger whose knee is three times the size it was when she boarded.

T he meal cart slammed into it! I hope that the flight attendant said she was sorry. They say that the swelling usually goes down within five to seven days. Or is it five to seven years?

FLIGHT ATTENDANTS DON'T NEED . . .

The passenger asking them, "Remember us? You were on our flight to Orlando last winter!"

S ometimes flight attendants say, "Yes, I remember you," even if they don't. Sometimes they say "Yes, I remember you," even if it was 13 months, 407 flights, and 66,000 passengers ago.

THE LAST THING A FLIGHT ATTENDANT WANTS IS A LATE CHECK-IN AT THE AIRPORT AND . . .

The passenger who sits in 7-C stowing his lunchbox-size carry-on in the overhead bin, closing the bin and then telling every other passenger opening the bin, "That is my bin."

If the bin is not full, leave it open for your co-passengers' belongings. The flight attendants will close them as they become full. Everyone must share the bin space and there isn't much bin space left these days. Is it really $17 for the first piece of checked luggage and $65 for the second?

ALL THAT A FLIGHT ATTENDANT NEEDS IS ANOTHER CUT IN PAY AND . . .

Another passenger asking the male flight attendant, "Did you buy that tie?"

M ost airline uniforms include a tie issued by the uniform company. The management gets upset when the flight attendant offers to sell it to a passenger for $35! Would the management have selected that tie if they had to wear it to work every day? The same tie every day!

JUST WHAT EVERY FLIGHT ATTENDANT NEEDS . . .

The lavatory passenger who just denied that he was smoking in there even though the smoke detector is blasting and smoke is too thick to cut with a crash axe.

P lease don't even think of doing this. Can you imagine a fire on an airplane? One would not live long enough to spend time in jail or pay the fine.

ONE MORE EXCUSE FOR A FLIGHT ATTENDANT'S BAD ATTITUDE IS . . .

A sponge that is approximately 2 1/2 inches by 3 inches that is included in the life raft equipment.

Is this little sponge really going to keep the raft dry out in the middle of the ocean?

FLIGHT ATTENDANTS DON'T NEED . . .

The passenger seated in 9-F next to the engine on the Airbus asking, "What is that noise?"

The engine is just outside your window. By the time we land, in two hours and forty minutes, you will probably be deaf. Do you think the designers of these airplanes have ever actually ridden on them?

THE LAST THING A FLIGHT ATTENDANT WANTS IS A LATE CHECK-IN AT THE AIRPORT AND . . .

The passenger asking the flight attendant just after the entry door has been closed, "How do you know that everyone is on?"

Hint: Because every seat is occupied. Why do passengers care?

ALL THAT A FLIGHT ATTENDANT NEEDS IS ANOTHER CUT IN PAY AND . . .

One more passenger asking, "Can I take a box of tissues and this meal tray home?"

Please don't. Stores sell that size tissue box for $1.09, and I bet that bright green meal tray really wouldn't match anything in your dining room. If you do, flight attendants will take another seven percent cut in pay.

JUST WHAT EVERY FLIGHT ATTENDANT NEEDS . . .

One more flight attendant manual printed with two full pages explaining how to brew coffee.

D oes anyone wonder why the newly hired flight attendants come onto the aircraft for the first time so intimidated by the coffee maker? (1) Place coffee filter into tray. (2) Push the "on" button. (3) Push the "brew" button. Three sentences should do it.

ONE MORE EXCUSE FOR A FLIGHT ATTENDANT'S BAD ATTITUDE IS . . .

Once into the raft, the flight attendant realizes that none of the flares are working and that the signaling mirror was taken off that aircraft last month by her roommate to use for her makeup.

D on't believe this. The equipment on those rafts is regularly checked by the FAA. Besides, if you saw her roommate, you would know that she hasn't used a mirror for her makeup in years!

PAYING PASSENGERS
REALLY DON'T WANT . . .

One more flight attendant screaming at them that their laptop computer should have been turned off and stowed ten minutes ago!

Do these rules really apply to everyone or is this person just too important to follow the rules? If one has really flown that many miles and is that important, please start setting a better example for the others. What does "important" really mean?

FLIGHT ATTENDANTS
DON'T NEED . . .

Thirty-nine blankets covering the megaphone when the FAA is on board inspecting the overhead bins.

The FAA gets so upset when items are placed on top of the emergency equipment. Please, no coats on top of those big yellow life rafts. Wouldn't it be a mess to relocate all of those garments just to get the raft out of the bin, inflate the raft and throw it into the ocean? Listen, the airline is not going to replace a passenger's $19,000 fur coat when it lands in the water!

THE LAST THING A FLIGHT ATTENDANT WANTS IS A LATE CHECK-IN AT THE AIRPORT AND . . .

A 103-year-old passenger asking for cranberry sauce!

Oh sir, do you mean cranberry juice? Well, it doesn't matter. Cranberry anything really keeps you cleaned out. We admire those senior citizens that still enjoy traveling. Many of them are younger than today's flight attendants.

~

ALL THAT A FLIGHT ATTENDANT NEEDS IS ANOTHER CUT IN PAY AND . . .

One more mother asking, "Don't you have a juice box for my child?"

No kiddie juice boxes on airplanes. Hint: Give the flight attendant your baby bottle; the flight attendant will rinse it out and fill it with apple juice. Airlines don't show a profit. How could they afford juice boxes?

JUST WHAT EVERY FLIGHT ATTENDANT NEEDS . . .

Another passenger who thinks it is time to use the lavatory just when the seat belt sign is turned on.

If it really is an emergency, let the flight attendants know. Most of are reasonable adults. Is there something in that seat belt chime that makes one need to go?

ONE MORE EXCUSE FOR A FLIGHT ATTENDANT'S BAD ATTITUDE IS . . .

Lasagna up to the elbows and a passenger commenting, "You guys are like on vacation all the time, aren't you?"

Flight attendants get to leave home but they do not get paid until they leave home. Well, they don't get paid until the engines are turned on. Well, in the case of a delay, sometimes they don't get paid for six hours after they have left home. "Industry Standard"?

FLIGHT ATTENDANTS DON'T NEED . . .

To walk in on the third passenger this week who has not locked the lavatory door.

Flight attendants are used to this; it is only embarrassing for passengers. Before one sits down in there, simply slide that little knob on the door, usually to the left. That should turn on the lights and lock you in there. If not, just leave the door open. Flight attendants really don't care.

~~~~~

THE LAST THING A FLIGHT ATTENDANT WANTS IS A LATE CHECK-IN AT THE AIRPORT AND . . .

A three-hour delay, followed by a hit by a de-icing truck causing $65,000 in damage to the wing.

How do airlines ever make money? Oh, I guess they don't, do they!

ALL THAT A FLIGHT
ATTENDANT NEEDS IS
ANOTHER CUT IN PAY AND . . .

The passenger who asks, "Can't I take off this clear plastic cover on the magazine and take this magazine with me?"

Sure, just give the airline one more excuse for losing money again this year. Please don't steal magazines, toilet paper, tissue, soap, or pillows from the airplanes. The airlines really are trying to show a profit.

JUST WHAT EVERY FLIGHT
ATTENDANT NEEDS . . .

The passenger who is staring at the sign above the jumpseat that reads, "For flight attendant use only," and asks, "Can I sit there?"

Come on, prove the flight attendants wrong; you can read. Right? Don't even ask most flight attendants this question. Some may just kill you!

ONE MORE EXCUSE FOR A FLIGHT ATTENDANT'S BAD ATTITUDE IS . . .

Their ability to only be assigned trips that take them away from home for nine days at a time.

You see, the senior flight attendants traditionally work trips that bring them back home every night. Would one really prefer trips that require them to be gone from home for nine days? Relationships are difficult in this industry!

FLIGHT ATTENDANTS DON'T NEED . . .

One more pilot who locks himself out of the cockpit.

That's okay. We were delayed for one hour waiting for the aircraft to be catered. What is another hour delay waiting to get into the cockpit? Two hours have now passed in which crew members are not paid. That's okay.

THE LAST THING THAT A FLIGHT ATTENDANT WANTS IS A LATE CHECK-IN AT THE AIRPORT AND . . .

One more passenger looking at the OCCU-PIED sign on the lavatory door and asking, "Is there someone in here?"

VACANT usually indicates that the room is empty and OCCUPIED usually indicates that there is someone in there. But here's the secret: About fifty percent of the time someone is in there when the VACANT sign is showing. When you go in there, flip the latch or don't be surprised if someone walks in on you.

ALL THAT A FLIGHT ATTENDANT NEEDS IS ANOTHER CUT IN PAY AND . . .

A first-class passenger who ate four of the hot entreés and thinks he has food poisoning.

Food poisoning on an airplane? Prove it! On a cruise ship, maybe! Four hot entreés?

JUST WHAT EVERY FLIGHT ATTENDANT NEEDS . . .

Another new mother asking if she can change her infant's diaper on your jumpseat.

Certainly. Don't worry about the smell that will filter down to row fifteen, into the galley, and into the cockpit. Just think about this: diaper changing on dirty jumpseats. The jumpseats are older than the airplane, just like some of the filght attendants!

ONE MORE EXCUSE FOR A FLIGHT ATTENDANT'S BAD ATTITUDE IS . . .

An aircraft that has finally reached the de-icing pad after a forty-five-minute wait and a planeload of passengers who need to use the lavatory.

The pad is the location where the aircraft is sprayed to remove ice and snow from the aircraft. Now the lavatories smell like deicing fluid. Just lock yourself in there!

THE LAST THING A FLIGHT ATTENDANT WANTS IS A LATE CHECK-IN AT THE AIRPORT AND . . .

One more passenger asking, "What do those little pink, yellow and blue lights up on the ceiling mean?"

These lights are mentioned on a least six written tests during a flight attendant's initial training class. Pink comes on when either the pilots call the flight attendants or when the flight attendants call each other. Yellow lights up when a passenger pushes the call button in the lavatory. Blue is the passenger call light indicating that a passenger wants something to eat, drink, a pillow, blanket, oxygen or the flight attendant to toss the dirty diaper. Please don't ever push that button!

FLIGHT ATTENDANTS DON'T NEED . . .

Passengers asking, "Why do you get shoulder harnesses on your jumpseat and we don't?"

I guess the airline just thinks that much of us. Or is it the aircraft manufacturer?

ALL THAT A FLIGHT ATTENDANT NEEDS IS ANOTHER CUT IN PAY AND . . .

A review of the section of the Airline Emergency Procedures manual entitled, "Dealing with Sharks."

Passengers, please listen to and take the safety information demonstration very seriously. Those sharks can be huge. When it comes down to dealing with sharks in the ocean, don't you think the airline expects too much of its flight attendants?

JUST WHAT EVERY FLIGHT ATTENDANT NEEDS . . .

An overweight passenger seated in the bulkhead seat.

The bulkhead seats, located behind a dividing wall, are usually the narrowest seats on the aircraft. If a passenger weighs much over seventy-seven pounds, he had better ask for another seat. The leg room is great, however the width of the seat is only ideal for a four-year-old. Have the people who designed these airplanes ever sat in them?

ONE MORE EXCUSE FOR A FLIGHT ATTENDANT'S BAD ATTITUDE IS . . .

The realization that the whistle is missing from the raft!

This is a signaling device to use when one is in the raft in the middle of the ocean. There must be someone in that raft with a whistle.

FLIGHT ATTENDANTS DON'T NEED . . .

A passenger staring at a bin full of pillows telling them that all of the bins are full.

It really is okay for a passenger to ask the flight attendant to remove the pillows from the bin to make room for their belongings. Was it in recent years that one last saw a bin full of pillows? Hint: Everyone bring your own!

ALL THAT A FLIGHT ATTENDANT NEEDS IS ANOTHER CUT IN PAY AND . . .

The realization that the number one item in their flight attendant manual under "Life Raft Operation" is "Keep raft dry!"

Now, who believes that? One is floating in a little raft with forty-seven other people in the middle of the ocean. The raft is equipped with a bailing bucket that would hold about one pint of liquid. Yes, let's keep it dry!

JUST WHAT EVERY FLIGHT ATTENDANT NEEDS ...

One more passenger asking, "Is A the window or the aisle seat?"

Aren't those drawings located below the bins stupid? They read "C-B-A" with a picture of a person next to the "C" and a picture of a window next to the "A." Could those aircraft designers have put them in alphabetical order?

ONE MORE EXCUSE FOR A FLIGHT ATTENDANT'S BAD ATTITUDE IS ...

Another passenger asking if there is a baby-changing table on board. When your answer is "no," and the passenger proceeds to change her newborn on your beverage cart.

Isn't this similar to using the kitchen table as a changing table just before sitting down to dinner? Oh, don't worry about it. Many of the beverage carts have not been cleaned for ten years or more.

FLIGHT ATTENDANTS
DON'T NEED . . .

Another passenger asking if their carry-on bag, which is three times larger than the bin, will fit into the bin.

"**M**ake my day," says the flight attendant. It is amazing that people who run companies and corporations really think that something three times larger will actually fit into these relatively small bins. Amazing but entertaining!

ALL THAT A FLIGHT
ATTENDANT NEEDS IS
ANOTHER CUT IN PAY AND . . .

A reminder that the average sea has waves of twelve to eighteen feet in height and that one must "keep the passengers calm!"

Calm? Do you know that many flight attendants can't even swim? Are we even paid to swim?

THE LAST THING A FLIGHT ATTENDANT WANTS IS A LATE CHECK-IN AT THE AIRPORT AND . . .

The realization that during the midnight evacuation in Boise, the exterior emergency lights did not automatically illuminate after the slide was deployed.

Don't worry about the lights; they were just meant to illuminate the escape areas and allow everyone to see the ground from the aircraft. The aircraft is only about seventeen feet above the ground. Jump onto the slide and you will probably know when you get to the bottom. Hopefully, the bottom of the slide is close to the ground. When you get to the bottom, run like heck!

JUST WHAT EVERY FLIGHT ATTENDANT NEEDS . . .

A boarding passenger who pushes his boarding pass three inches from the flight attendant's face and asks, "Where is my seat?"

Hint: The seat number is usually the largest number on the boarding pass. The number is followed by a letter. On most aircraft, seats A-B-C are located on the right and D-E-F are located on the left as one walks toward the back of the aircraft. Watch your step as you proceed to your seat, as these aisles aren't getting any wider—although both the flight attendants and passengers are!

FLIGHT ATTENDANTS DON'T NEED . . .

The passenger seated in 2-C telling them that the overhead bin above row 1 is open.

Thank you for being so helpful. Did you really think no one saw this? That's okay. Some flight attendants need as much help as they can get. After all, many only fly 177 days per year!

ONE MORE EXCUSE FOR A FLIGHT ATTENDANT'S BAD ADDITUDE IS . . .

When putting the shoulder straps on while seated in the jumpseat, her hair wraps around the reel-style belts, resulting in her hair needing to be cut to release her.

Flight attendants, review the Uniform Standards section of the manual under "grooming." The management says that there is a reason for every item in that ninety-eight page section.

ALL THAT A FLIGHT ATTENDANT NEEDS IS ANOTHER CUT IN PAY AND . . .

A few wealthy relatives to help support them through their first ten years as a flight attendant.

Give that rich aunt and uncle a call. It doesn't matter that you have never met them. Remember, the airline expects you to inflate life rafts into the ocean and put out fires, and the starting pay is only about $1,254 per month—before taxes.

JUST WHAT EVERY FLIGHT ATTENDANT NEEDS . . .

A passenger who thinks he knows more about the aircraft than the head mechanic and who asks, "What kind of engines does this plane have?"

Flight attendants are impressed by all of those passengers who know so much about airplanes. Most of them have trouble getting gas into their own car!

~~~~~~~~~

FLIGHT ATTENDANTS DON'T NEED . . .

Passengers seated in the bulkhead row thinking that the area underneath their seat belongs to them for their carry-on stowage.

Remember, the bulkhead seats are those located behind a dividing wall, so passengers have extra leg room. However, all of the carry-on items must be placed in an overhead bin, usually about nine rows behind those seats! The area below their seats belong to the people in the row behind.

PAYING PASSENGERS
REALLY DON'T WANT . . .

The last row of seats being assigned to them while they require an aisle chair.

An aisle chair is a narrow wheelchair that fits down the aisle. Ticket agents, save a row closer to the front of the aircraft for these passengers. Wouldn't row ten be better than row twenty-nine? Is there a system to any of this?

THE LAST THING A FLIGHT
ATTENDANT WANTS IS
A LATE CHECK-IN AT
THE AIRPORT AND . . .

The realization that the inflation handle is not connected to the inflatable raft.

If the raft will not inflate it becomes a ninety-pound cushion that will probably sink. How about everyone inflating their life vests while on the aircraft rather than as they're leaving headed for icy twelve-foot waves? Where is that inflation handle anyway?

ALL THAT A FLIGHT ATTENDANT NEEDS IS ANOTHER CUT IN PAY AND . . .

A second full-time job.

Look at it like this: The second full-time job probably pays more than your position as a flight attendant, but which one is more fun? Why don't flight attendants ever quit? You can tell by looking at them that they don't!

JUST WHAT EVERY FLIGHT ATTENDANT NEEDS . . .

The eight-month pregnant passenger boarding with her doctor's note in hand saying, "The doctor says that I will be just fine."

Shall we deliver this child in the middle of the aisle or in the back galley? Let's move her to the aisle. Only about twenty-six inches wide, but at least the aisle is carpeted. When was the last time that carpet was shampooed?

ONE MORE EXCUSE FOR A FLIGHT ATTENDANT'S BAD ATTITUDE IS . . .

When pouring refills of coffee for the third time, the passenger six rows ahead is already waving his cup in the aisle.

Flight attendants will not forget a passenger. In the event that they run out of coffee by the time they reach your row, they will refill the pot. There is usually more coffee where that previous pot came from. Some flight attendants say that if they were ever required to serve cappuccino they would quit. Isn't it time for many of them to?

FLIGHT ATTENDANTS
DON'T NEED . . .

A passenger using three bottles of airline oxygen during the flight and then happily walking himself off the aircraft.

A flight attendant would never take a chance on the idea that the passenger is faking it. Once the person next to him says, "I think he needs oxygen," a flight attendant will remove the oxygen from its stowage, turn the bottle on, and he can sit with it until the aircraft has landed. Isn't it easier to administer the oxygen than try to explain to the family and the airline why you did not? Just use the oxygen.

ALL THAT A FLIGHT
ATTENDANT NEEDS IS
ANOTHER CUT IN PAY AND . . .

The reminder that when one swims through burning oil or gas, one does not inflate the life vest until out of the burning area.

Are we going to escape the burning area? Newly hired flight attendants are paid about $16 per hour. Swimming through a burning area?

THE LAST THING A FLIGHT ATTENDANT WANTS IS A LATE CHECK-IN AT THE AIRPORT AND . . .

One more broken tray table.

Passengers certainly get upset, and scared, when their tray table crashes into their lap at takeoff. Those latches pull out so frequently, one would think that a piece of velcro would be more secure than that little screw. Oh that's right, some of the airplanes only sell for $47 million.

JUST WHAT EVERY FLIGHT ATTENDANT NEEDS . . .

Six passengers assigned to three seats.

Just a little confusion here; no one has been double-seated in row fourteen. The aircraft is departing from gate fourteen. Could this really happen? Sometimes it does!

ONE MORE EXCUSE FOR A FLIGHT ATTENDANT'S BAD ATTITUDE IS . . .

The boarding passenger claims that her thirty-six-inch bag cannot be checked as it is full of her medication.

Guess what? She is 103 years old, traveling alone, and expects the flight attendant to lift her bag into the bin. Another flight attendant will be out of work with a back injury. Passengers, please pay the extra $700 and check those heavy bags.

FLIGHT ATTENDANTS DON'T NEED . . .

One more passenger asking, "How long have you been doing this and how old is this airplane?"

Curious I know, but there isn't much turnover in this career anymore. Some of these flight attendants are over 100, and many of them are much older than the planes!

ALL THAT A FLIGHT ATTENDANT NEEDS IS ANOTHER CUT IN PAY AND . . .

The passenger seated in 5-D, on a flight from Chicago to San Francisco, is asking for cappuccino.

A ren't six kinds of juice, six brands of beer, five types of pop, coffee and decaf enough to offer? Here's a secret: if the airline ever begins serving cappuccino, flight attendants will quit. You know they will!

JUST WHAT EVERY FLIGHT ATTENDANT NEEDS . . .

The passenger seated in 1-A asking the flight attendant if she will assist her in threading her needle.

T hat is just great that the airline allows the passengers to work on their craft projects during the flight. If flight attendants got out their craft project during a flight they would find themselves in a manager's office before the end of the week.

FLIGHT ATTENDANTS DON'T NEED . . .

A hideous-looking uniform scarf or tie.

Isn't it management that usually decides what the flight attendants wear? These items are expensive for an airline but can't the management narrow the choice to two and let the flight attendants vote on one? What happened to those flight attendant uniform committees anyway?

THE LAST THING A FLIGHT ATTENDANT WANTS IS A LATE CHECK-IN AT THE AIRPORT AND . . .

A full aircraft of passengers imitating you as you are doing the safety demonstration.

This is serious information. Imitate the flight attendants during this demonstration and just see who will assist you during an emergency evacuation!

ALL THAT A FLIGHT ATTENDANT NEEDS IS ANOTHER CUT IN PAY AND . . .

A passenger who decides during a water landing that he wants to use the flight attendant's designated pink life vest rather than his assigned orange vest.

Go ahead, take the flight attendant's pink vest! The other passengers will just think that he is a flight attendant and knows what he is doing. Although the aircraft engines are probably turned off while the aircraft is floating in the water, I think that the flight attendants are still getting paid. Or are they? Let the passengers do the work!

JUST WHAT EVERY FLIGHT ATTENDANT NEEDS . . .

145 passengers boarding with 279 holiday gifts to be stowed in the overhead bins.

Hint: Next year, use a package delivery service to send your gifts to your loved ones. By next year, that delivery service charge will cost less than the extra checked or carry-on baggage charge by the airlines. Your travel experience will be more enjoyable, and you will avoid "that look" from the flight attendants. You know the look!

FLIGHT ATTENDANTS DON'T NEED . . .

One more passenger asking, "Do you get to fly free on your days off?"

The answer is "yes" it is called standby. With fewer airlines and airplanes in the air today, it can be very difficult to fly free. It's just easier to stay home.

ONE MORE EXCUSE FOR A FLIGHT ATTENDANT'S BAD ATTITUDE IS . . .

To learn that 10,000 flights are going to be cancelled because the pilots are going to go on strike.

On strike again? Do the pilots, airline and union care if 1,397,000 passengers never come back? Oh we know, by next month those passengers will have forgotten how the pilots, airline and union messed up their vacation for the year. It is just an "industry standard"!

PAYING PASSENGERS REALLY DON'T WANT . . .

One more flight attendant contradicting the ticket agent who just told them that they could bring on their refrigerator!

Let's be reasonable about this, folks. The average refrigerator measures 65" by 32". Aren't those overhead bins about 25" by 30"? No refrigerators please!

THE LAST THING A FLIGHT ATTENDANT WANTS IS A LATE CHECK-IN AT THE AIRPORT AND . . .

A mechanic telling the pilot, "This will be an easy fix," after you have already experienced a six-hour delay.

How does an airline ever make money when it pays for hotel rooms for 147 passengers, each requiring two meals during the delay? If one wants to lose $20 million quickly, invest in an airline.

JUST WHAT EVERY FLIGHT ATTENDANT NEEDS . . .

After 17 years of flying and having submitted 269 suggestions to the airline, the flight attendant has never seen one of his/her suggestions used.

Why is it that, at many companies, the management team asks for employee suggestions, but seldom implements them? The designers of these aircraft don't know that they've made design errors; it's the flight attendants who make them work.

ALL THAT A FLIGHT ATTENDANT NEEDS IS ANOTHER CUT IN PAY AND . . .

Having to teach one more passenger the difference between the ashtray and the door handle located on the lavatory door.

No smoking allowed on the aircraft! Yes, airplanes are still constructed with ashtrays. But don't even think about it! Oh yes, the ashtray usually pulls right off the door. Next time, please replace the ashtray or let the flight attendant do it. Don't just leave it on the floor. Thank you!

ONE MORE EXCUSE FOR A FLIGHT ATTENDANT'S BAD ATTITUDE IS . . .

When the In-Flight department announces that the airline will be receiving another new type of aircraft requiring another fourteen hours of "transition training," for which the company will pay you seven hours.

Seven hours of pay for fourteen hours of work! If one did not work an airline, would one consider this to be normal? Flight attendants do! This is "industry standard." Wouldn't you like to meet the person that set these standards?

FLIGHT ATTENDANTS DON'T NEED . . .

The passenger seated in 1-D asking, "Can we just see the slide one time?"

Do you think that this slide, installed on each door and used in the case of an evacuation, resembles that of an amusement park slide? Not close; it is only about fourteen feet long. I hope that I never have to see it!

THE LAST THING A FLIGHT ATTENDANT WANTS IS A LATE CHECK-IN AT THE AIRPORT AND . . .

One more passenger refusing to check her carry-on bag measuring fifty-six inches because all of her jewelry and medication is in there.

J ust leave the jewelry at home where the thieves have easy access to it and cut back on some of that medication. Is anyone really going to break into your twenty-fifth-floor condo while you are away for the winter?

ALL THAT A FLIGHT ATTENDANT NEEDS IS ANOTHER CUT IN PAY AND . . .

The realization that the passenger at the baggage claim has not one, but two first-class navy blue airline blankets that she did not pay for.

Would you go to northern Michigan in December not expecting it to be five degrees below zero? How about knitting a nice warm sweater during that seventeen-hour delay earlier in the day? Please don't remove blankets from the aircraft unless you have paid for them. Oh well. How often are those blankets cleaned anyway?

JUST WHAT EVERY FLIGHT ATTENDANT NEEDS ...

The forward jumpseat of the one-year-old aircraft suddenly falls off the wall while the flight attendant is seated on it!

What can one expect today? Many of these new airplanes cost less than $50 million! Is it the construction of the aircraft, or is it the increased weight of the flight attendants? I don't know.

FLIGHT ATTENDANTS DON'T NEED ...

To question themselves one more time after they have been secured into their jumpseats that everything is locked down and secured in the galley.

Big deal? You bet it is. Imagine one of those 250-pound beverage carts getting loose upon landing. Don't worry about the 300-pound flight attendant getting loose, either.

THE LAST THING A FLIGHT ATTENDANT WANTS IS A LATE CHECK-IN AT THE AIRPORT AND . . .

A passenger trying to open the entry door while they are at 37,000 feet.

Many people think that the entry door is actually the lavatory door. No, it is not the closet door either. The lavatory is the next door with the little latch, indicating VACANT or OCCUPIED. The aircraft would get too cold if the entry door were opened at 37,000 feet!

ALL THAT A FLIGHT ATTENDANT NEEDS IS ANOTHER CUT IN PAY AND . . .

To be told by the airline that they must bring their own hanger from home to hang their uniform blazer in the elevating coat closet.

Forget about the hanger! The $195 uniform blazer, which retails for $79 anyplace else can be thrown into an overhead bin for nine hours. A hanger from home?

JUST WHAT EVERY FLIGHT ATTENDANT NEEDS . . .

One more 10-year-old passenger acting like a sweet, innocent child.

Flight attendants enjoy seeing the sweet and inno-cent children on the airplane. Flight attendants would appreciate it if the parents would do as their children do: Buckle the seat belt, put the tray table up when asked, even turn off the iPod and cell phone when asked. Why is this so hard for parents? Children usually even say thank you!

FLIGHT ATTENDANTS DON'T NEED . . .

Just one more trip where they fall asleep on their jumpseats during takeoff.

How could one fall asleep on those stiff, narrow, flat, poorly designed jumpseats? Easily, when a flight attendant has been scheduled for a seventeen-hour day. (Just another "industry standard.")

ONE MORE EXCUSE FOR A FLIGHT ATTENDANT'S BAD ATTITUDE IS . . .

The discovery that the airline has just ordered ten new airplanes that are twenty-four feet shorter than the current airplanes. However, they will seat the same number of passengers as the current aircraft.

Oh, who will ever notice! These airlines have been putting the squeeze on their passengers for years. It won't help those over five feet tall, but it may provide the reason to lose those sixty-five pounds. Remember to thank the airline when you do!

THE LAST THING A FLIGHT ATTENDANT WANTS IS A LATE CHECK-IN AT THE AIRPORT AND . . .

Malfunctioning batteries on the defibrillator.

G reat! Neither of the batteries are operating. Make an announcement asking if there is a doctor or nurse on board or if any passenger is carrying a defibrillator! If no luck, tell the captain that you would suggest a quick emergency landing. Then plan to quit the job tomorrow.

ALL THAT A FLIGHT ATTENDANT NEEDS IS ANOTHER CUT IN PAY AND . . .

A good union representative.

M any airlines have unions representing their flight attendants and they pay between $500 – $700 per year in union dues. Now this really is an "industry standard," isn't it?

JUST WHAT EVERY FLIGHT ATTENDANT NEEDS . . .

The passenger seated in 5-C showing the flight attendant that he has brought on his own CPR mask.

Flight attendants, don't be stupid about this. Start looking for a doctor, nurse or emergency medial technician. Don't even wait!

FLIGHT ATTENDANTS DON'T NEED . . .

Forgetful crew schedulers.

Sometimes flight attendants check in at 5 a.m. only to learn that the flight is delayed until 8 a.m. They got up at 3 a.m.! No pay until 8 a.m. Just another "industry standard."

THE LAST THING A FLIGHT ATTENDANT WANTS IS A LATE CHECK-IN AT THE AIRPORT AND . . .

Another passenger leaving the lavatory saying, "You need more toilet paper in there!"

I need more toilet paper in there? Flight attendants will be happy to get more toilet paper in there. Just remember to flush!

ALL THAT A FLIGHT ATTENDANT NEEDS IS ANOTHER CUT IN PAY AND . . .

One more passenger asking if there is coconut milk on the airplane.

It is unfortunate that many airlines don't even carry milk today. Guess what? There aren't any refrigerators, microwaves or ice machines on $47 million airplanes! Coconut milk on an airplane?

JUST WHAT EVERY FLIGHT ATTENDANT NEEDS . . .

A plastic surgeon after twelve years of flying.

Even the finest conditions on these airplanes are pretty poor. You think that flight attendant is only fifty-five? Guess again.

~~~~~

ONE MORE EXCUSE FOR A FLIGHT ATTENDANT'S BAD ATTTITUDE IS . . .

Having to advise another passenger to remove the paper napkin that he pushed up into the reading lamp to block out the light because he cannot get the light switch to work.

You know what? Those reading light bulbs get extremely hot. Please don't put the napkins into the light fixture. No one wants a fire on an airplane. You will have to wait until you get home to sleep. If flight attendants can't sleep on the airplane, passengers probably shouldn't either.

FLIGHT ATTENDANTS DON'T NEED . . .

Another passenger asking, "Can I keep these cups and napkins for landing? I have a bloody nose."

T he worst. Blood everywhere! The poor guy's nose bled until the paramedics met the airplane. No one told you about this in the interview, did they?

ALL THAT A FLIGHT ATTENDANT NEEDS IS ANOTHER CUT IN PAY AND . . .

The gate agent asking if they should board the obnoxious and loud couple who have been drinking since last December!

A gents, you must be kidding. Send them back to their hotel and tell them that there is another flight next week. Agents, if you send those passengers on the aircraft, you are going to ride with them!

JUST WHAT EVERY FLIGHT ATTENDANT NEEDS . . .

A crystal ball.

Great! Flight attendants are asked twenty times each week, "What river is that down there?" Flight attendants seldom look out the window. They are just too busy getting another glass of water, another pillow, cup of coffee or air sick bag. Why don't they know those rivers by name?

JUST WHAT EVERY FLIGHT ATTENDANT NEEDS . . .

Another passenger leaping out of the back lavatory completely naked!

No wonder flight attendants often feel that they are on someone's candid camera! Is it the high price of gasoline, the long lines at the airports or global warming? Has most everyone just stepped out of the box a little too far? Or just the lavatory?

ONE MORE EXCUSE FOR A FLIGHT ATTENDANT'S BAD ATTITUDE IS . . .

Another new aircraft designed with the center aisle only one inch wider than the 250-pound beverage cart.

O h, and would it be interesting if the designers of these aircraft had to actually work in the aisle. Narrow seats, narrow aisles, wasted closet space, and no room for all of that trash. Now, the In-Flight department wants flight attendants to do an additional beverage and snack service resulting in more trash!

FLIGHT ATTENDANTS DON'T NEED . . .

Another mature adult passenger that never says "thank you" when they place his requested beverage on his tray table.

F light attendants see this every day. Why is it that children under ten years old almost always say "thank you"?

THE LAST THING A FLIGHT ATTENDANT WANTS IS A LATE CHECK-IN AT THE AIRPORT AND . . .

Another passenger asking, "Which side is F on?"

D on't make any of this too difficult. As one is headed down the aisle the seats are in alphabetical order beginning with 'A' on the right by the window going through 'F' over to the other window; providing the aircraft has six seats across. Why would 'F' ever be on the aisle?

ALL THAT A FLIGHT ATTENDANT NEEDS IS ANOTHER CUT IN PAY AND . . .

A new requirement by the airline to sell candy and other snacks in the aisle to try to make up for current company losses.

W hy didn't the airlines start raising their fares five years ago? Are the airlines scared that they might show a profit? Who are their CFOs?

JUST WHAT EVERY FLIGHT ATTENDANT NEEDS . . .

Another memo from the airline outlining the "zero tolerance" policy for abusive and violent passenger behavior.

Zero tolerance? The passenger paid for the seat, and now he owns the airline. Some flight attendants think this is true. Perhaps, simply: Not true!

ONE MORE EXCUSE FOR A FLIGHT ATTENDANT'S BAD ATTITUDE IS . . .

For the fifth time this week, there's a run on seat belt extensions.

The aircraft is equipped with only ten seat belt extensions. When they're all in use, the airline faces a delay in the departure time to obtain additional extensions. Perhaps the airlines should take some of that food off the aircraft. Oh, they already have! Good, now we have room for more extensions.

FLIGHT ATTENDANTS
DON'T NEED . . .

Newspaper headlines that read: "Complaints on the Part of Airline Passengers Are at All Time High!"

Complaints? The check-in and security lines are longer than ever; the seats are smaller than ever; double-seating is more common than ever; the meals, pillows and blankets are expensive. Complaints? Oh, and the flight attendants are older than ever!

THE LAST THING A FLIGHT
ATTENDANT WANTS IS
A LATE CHECK-IN AT
THE AIRPORT AND . . .

One more gate agent telling them that a party of four has been drinking in the gate area for the past two hours, but they should be fine once they get into the air.

Party of four, please come back to the airport in about a month! Drinking and flying just don't go together for a lot of people. Is it really okay that not everyone has flown before?

126

ALL THAT A FLIGHT ATTENDANT NEEDS IS ANOTHER CUT IN PAY AND . . .

One more passenger seated in first class asking if he can have another cocktail just after the entry door has been closed and we are ready for take-off.

Whoever decided that 'pre-departure beverages' served in first class during the boarding process was a good idea must be nuts! Today these passengers want two or three drinks within the first ten minutes of being seated. Perhaps it's time for liquor to be removed from the aircraft.

JUST WHAT EVERY FLIGHT ATTENDANT NEEDS . . .

Turn the lavatories into closets.

Airplanes never have enough space for carry-on luggage. Use the lavatories in the terminal and the aircraft could be constructed with three more closets. The closets would be a lot cleaner!

FLIGHT ATTENDANTS
DON'T NEED . . .

Another young mother asking them, "How do you suggest I change my baby?"

If the aircraft does not have a changing table in the lavatory, just back into that three-foot-wide lavatory and change the baby on your lap. Oh, please don't come out expecting to hand the dirty diaper to the flight attendant. Place it in the trash container located to the right of the sink. Flight attendants have this job so they won't have to deal with their own children's diapers.

ALL THAT A FLIGHT
ATTENDANT NEEDS IS
ANOTHER CUT IN PAY AND . . .

A passenger (or another flight attendant) who is a human time bomb!

After twelve days of flying, some flight attendants are about to explode. Is it the passengers, the airline, the spouse or the children at home? What is it anyway?

THE LAST THING A FLIGHT ATTENDANT WANTS IS A LATE CHECK-IN AT THE AIRPORT AND . . .

A memo from catering indicating that the flight attendants will now only serve crackers on the four-hour flights.

Passengers, pack a sandwich, salad, orange and a cookie on most flights today. Although the cost of fuel, oil and salaries has increased over the past fifteen years, airline tickets were higher ten or fifteen years ago. And why are airlines losing money?

JUST WHAT EVERY FLIGHT ATTENDANT NEEDS . . .

A passenger interfering with the job by pushing them into the beverage cart.

Most flight attendants are just trying to serve a meal, pour some pop and stay out of trouble. It is not a good idea to interfere with the operation of a flight attendant, on or off the job!

ONE MORE EXCUSE FOR A FLIGHT ATTENDANT'S BAD ATTITUDE IS . . .

To come home from a five-day trip only to find that a fellow flight attendant has trimmed their white toy poodle and spraypainted it pink!

Is it any wonder that some flight attendants won't follow the airline's uniform regulations? Earrings, for example, are required to be hoops no larger than the size of a quarter. Some of these hoops are the size of dog collars! Don't ever ask a flight attendant to trim your poodle.

FLIGHT ATTENDANTS DON'T NEED . . .

Twenty-two passengers putting on the oxygen masks that have dropped from the overhead compartments after a rough landing.

Don't touch the masks. It was just a rough landing. Now, the mechanics and flight crew will deal with the repair of two flat tires and another six-hour unpaid delay.

ALL THAT A FLIGHT ATTENDANT NEEDS IS ANOTHER CUT IN PAY AND . . .

The realization that they will drop 1,465 seniority numbers if the other airline buys yours.

D on't worry, you won't lose your job, yet. The union contract doesn't expire for another nine months, so your salary won't take a plunge until then. You will be required to work nineteen days per month instead of the eleven that you work now, and you will never see a weekend off again. Don't worry, you will be able to keep your job!

JUST WHAT EVERY FLIGHT ATTENDANT NEEDS . . .

A brand new aircraft that still comes equipped with those same "No Smoking/Fasten Seat Belt" signs.

It just isn't a good idea for anyone to smoke on a airplane; it means a big fine and way too much time in jail. That "Fasten Seat Belt" sign applies to everyone; even frequent fliers. Everyone buckle up; it really is a good idea!

FLIGHT ATTENDANTS DON'T NEED . . .

One more passenger asking, "Did you make the coffee?"

It really does not matter who pushed the brew button. It DOES matter when the water lines freeze on the aircraft and the flight attendants are unable to make the coffee!

THE LAST THING A FLIGHT ATTENDANT WANTS IS A LATE CHECK-IN AT THE AIRPORT AND . . .

A passenger who asks, "Are you still with this airline?"

U nlike other professions, there is not a lot of turn-over within the flight attendant industry. Where else can you get eighteen days off per month and make $59,000 per year? When doing three-day trips, one may only have to drive to work four times per month. How stupid do you think those flight attendants are?

ALL THAT A FLIGHT ATTENDANT NEEDS IS ANOTHER CUT IN PAY AND . . .

To have your flight attendant manager call you at home to ask you to participate in a "mini-evacuation," which will be conducted by the FAA, on the airline's newest aircraft.

G uess what, this participation is voluntary! No pay! The FAA wants to know that the flight attendants can evacuate passengers out of the new aircraft in the case of an emergency. The airline can afford to send their executives to a meeting in Hawaii for a week but not pay the flight attendants for the "mini-evac." I guess this makes sense.

JUST WHAT EVERY FLIGHT ATTENDANT NEEDS . . .

A new flight attendant from another airline telling you how they used to do it.

Y ou know what, that other airline is probably out of business or they would not be here. Please, please, please, just leave that previous airline stuff back at the previous airline. Isn't it just amazing how so many airlines go belly up and then reappear?

JUST WHAT EVERY FLIGHT ATTENDANT NEEDS . . .

The airline to offer the flight attendants a "free first-class" travel pass for perfect attendance over the next ninety days!

T hese airlines certainly don't want anyone using their sick time, do they? A "free first-class" standby travel pass! Every seat is full. One would be 105 years old before they ever got on! If a flight attendant used the sick time for even forty hours they would probably make about $1,500. How stupid does one think the flight attendants are? Let's see, $1,500 or a "free" travel pass?

FLIGHT ATTENDANTS DON'T NEED . . .

The next series of new aircraft delivered with even larger overhead bins which will accommodate even larger and heavier carry-on bags.

Any idea how many flight attendants require back surgery every year due to lifting bags brought onto the aircraft? Dear Passenger, no matter how large or how heavy the bag is, or how old you are, if you cannot place that bag into the overhead bin and remove it yourself, please don't bring it aboard. Isn't it only $25 or $30 to check it?

THE LAST THING A FLIGHT ATTENDANT WANTS IS A LATE CHECK-IN AT THE AIRPORT AND . . .

One more passenger asking, "Is it fun to go down that slide?"

I t is probably as much fun as a train wreck! It is only about fourteen feet long and bounces around a lot. Can't you just see 159 overweight passengers evacuating the aircraft via this narrow slide? I hope that I never have to see it!

ALL THAT A FLIGHT ATTENDANT NEEDS IS ANOTHER CUT IN PAY AND . . .

Three more pages added to their flight attendant manual covering "how to remove the lavatory doors in the event of door latch failure."

O h, those lavatory doors! Yes, sometimes they come loose and fall off, but don't worry. Among the other 17,000 items that flight attendants are trained on, lavatory door repair is one of them. Don't you really think that they expect too much of us?

JUST WHAT EVERY FLIGHT ATTENDANT NEEDS . . .

One more article that states that regularly scheduled flights were late, delayed or cancelled forty percent of the time last year.

Don't passengers expect way too much sometimes? A three-hour late arrival: Was that business meeting that important? A six-hour delay: The airline just gave out meal vouchers! Flight cancelled: Come back tomorrow when there will be 300 more passengers waiting for those same 150 seats.

FLIGHT ATTENDANTS DON'T NEED . . .

One more passenger who gets up when the seat belt sign is on.

Folks, the seat belt sign is on for everyone. Whether this is your first flight or you fly fifty-two weeks each year, anyone can get hurt. Most airlines are out of lawsuit money!

ONE MORE EXCUSE FOR A FLIGHT ATTENDANT'S BAD ATTITUDE IS . . .

One more "write up" for the mechanics to repair an armrest, a seat back and a tray table on the aircraft that you have just worked on for the past ten hours.

Most flight attendants look at these write-ups as just one more hassle, but someone has to do it. When flight attendants are hired, they all tell the interviewer that they would be happy to do lots of write-ups, restock lavatories, dump garbage, clean seats, put out fires and break up fights. Why don't flight attendants ever quit?

FLIGHT ATTENDANTS DON'T NEED . . .

To be reminded that when working Door 2-R they are responsible for everything back there.

2-R indicates Door 2 on the right hand side in the back of the aircraft. That flight attendant is responsible for the activities during an evacuation, plus selling a lot of junk during the flight and turning on the ovens and pressing the brew button on the coffee maker! There is a lot more to a flight attendant's job than serving a meal and beverage!

ONE MORE EXCUSE FOR A FLIGHT ATTENDANT'S BAD ATTITUDE IS . . .

Forty-seven headphones that do not work.

Oh, don't expect so much! Passengers need to start bring their own iPod, CD player or DVD player.

THE LAST THING A FLIGHT ATTENDANT WANTS IS A LATE CHECK-IN AT THE AIRPORT AND . . .

After the life-vest demonstration, another passenger asking, "What body of water would we be landing in between Denver and Phoenix?"

Don't worry about the body of water. This is what flight attendants are trained to do. Most just want to do a good job and mind their own business. Just remember that the life vest is in a little pouch under the seat. Do not inflate the vest while on the aircraft!

ALL THAT A FLIGHT ATTENDANT NEEDS IS ANOTHER CUT IN PAY AND . . .

The discovery that signing up to work at the door in the back of the aircraft means that they are in charge of monitoring the Waste System Quantity Indicator for the next five days.

This is almost as gross as it sounds. The amount of waste in the lavatory tank can be verified by the flight attendant on a quantity indicator. When the waste tank becomes full, a light will illuminate and all of the lavatories toilets will be inoperative. This is a problem! And you thought that all flight attendants do is serve food and beverage!

JUST WHAT EVERY FLIGHT
ATTENDANT NEEDS . . .

One more flight attendant who is even stranger than the passenger seated in 15-D.

G oing to a party with fifty other flight attendants is a very scary experience. It is even more frightful when one believes that all of these flight attendants are normal. How many flight attendants do you know?

FLIGHT ATTENDANTS
DON'T NEED . . .

To read one more newspaper's cover story, "Airline Service Report Cards."

F light attendants are primarily on board for passengers' safety, but is that an excuse for no service? How many passengers have been on a five-hour flight and seen the flight attendants in the aisle only one time? Did they leave through the back doors?

ALL THAT A FLIGHT ATTENDANT NEEDS IS ANOTHER CUT IN PAY AND . . .

A review of the latest manual revision details, "What to do in the event of toilet flooding."

Bottom line here is to attend a good school for plumbers before applying to an airline. If the toilet floods, turn the water supply selector valve to the shut-off position. Toilet flooding can really be a mess if you have just departed from any city in Mexico!

FLIGHT ATTENDANTS DON'T NEED . . .

One more lesson and another skill sheet on "How to Remove Latex Gloves."

Who's complaining? At least now flight attendants have gloves on the aircraft for picking up all that garbage. It certainly is nice that the airline is offering free flu shots each winter.

JUST WHAT EVERY FLIGHT ATTENDANT NEEDS . . .

Another newspaper article reporting that the flights that they have worked for the past five years have been among the nation's one hundred worst airline flights for delays and cancellations.

The parking ramps are full, the security lines are too long, mechanics have one more repair to complete, catering has to return to the aircraft because of a 100-meal shortage and passengers can't find their gate. No, airlines do not cancel just because a small number of passengers have booked.

THE LAST THING A FLIGHT ATTENDANT WANTS IS A LATE CHECK-IN AT THE AIRPORT AND . . .

One more passenger about to pull the bi-fold lavatory door off its hinges by using the handle that reads, "push!"

The airplane is not like home. There is a little silver plaque near the center of the door that says "push." When one pushes in that general area, the door will open, allowing you to enter. If, by chance you "pull" on the door and it does come flying off its hinges, do not worry. Flight attendants have six pages in their manual explaining how to put the door back into working order.

ALL THAT A FLIGHT ATTENDANT NEEDS IS ANOTHER CUT IN PAY AND . . .

One more passenger complaining that their coupon book does not include the "free hot dog" coupon to be used in Las Vegas.

Coupons to be used for a free hot dog! In Las Vegas? Folks, you are about to lose $17,000 gambling. Forget the coupon and spend $1.59 for that hot dog. Oh, and on your return flight home, please don't take it out on the flight attendant that you lost it all and now can't make your next house payment.

JUST WHAT EVERY FLIGHT ATTENDANT NEEDS . . .

To remind the junior flight attendant of nine years that she is not in charge.

Some of these flight attendants certainly can be independent and bossy! With just nine years of seniority, she wants to tell the flight attendant with twenty years of seniority how to do the job. At nine years, she is still "on call," filling in for those that have the nerve to call in sick! Patience is required.

147

ONE MORE EXCUSE FOR A FLIGHT ATTENDANT'S BAD ATTITUDE IS . . .

Not one flight running on schedule within the past three weeks.

Just another unpaid delay. Flight attendants check in at 2 p.m. for the 3 p.m. departure, but don't learn about the delay until 2:30 p.m. The flight is now departing at 6 p.m. How many hours should one show up for work prior to getting paid? Wait time is not paid time—an "industry standard."

ALL THAT A FLIGHT ATTENDANT NEEDS IS ANOTHER CUT IN PAY AND . . .

The airline to implement one more "surcharge!"

Shouldn't airlines just raise the fares and drop the surcharges? Is there really a $3 usher fee to cover the cost of the flight attendant assisting the passenger to his seat?

THE LAST THING A FLIGHT ATTENDANT WANTS IS A LATE CHECK-IN AT THE AIRPORT AND . . .

One more passenger asking for Diet Dr. Pepper, when the airline doesn't even carry regular Dr. Pepper.

Why don't the airlines provide nineteen more beverages on those carts? The carts weight 250 pounds and already carry thirty-seven items. Perhaps the passengers should suggest to the airline what they would prefer to see on the carts. Why would an airline ever ask the flight attendants who deal with this every day?

PAYING PASSENGERS REALLY DON'T WANT . . .

Six out of eight lavatories "out of order" on the aircraft.

Just a mess and couldn't they make them a little smaller? Back into this thing if you weigh much more than 90 pounds. Please, wipe the sink and flush when finished. Pretend that you are at home!

JUST WHAT EVERY FLIGHT ATTENDANT NEEDS . . .

One more report from your company's spokesperson, "We are trying to improve."

Flight attendants try to show up on time, every day, for every flight. If they are late one minute, within a week they are seated in front of a management team member. Where did that expression "team member" come from?

~~~~~~

ONE MORE EXCUSE FOR A FLIGHT ATTENDANT'S BAD ATTITUDE IS . . .

The gate agent who tells them, "Good luck! No pass riders have gotten on this flight in three weeks."

The flight attendant is pass riding in order to get home. The flight attendant gets on. There are forty-nine vacant seats. Agents, start being nicer to those flight attendants. Don't take it out on them that you chose to work twenty-two days each month and they work eleven!

FLIGHT ATTENDANTS DON'T NEED . . .

Long on-board ground delays.

Has anyone ever been stuck on an airplane for ten hours, on the ground? There wasn't a crumb of food on that aircraft and there was only one gallon of water. Can't a catering truck get out there with some pizza and pop?

~~~~~~

THE LAST THING A FLIGHT ATTENDANT NEEDS IS A LATE CHECK-IN AT THE AIRPORT AND . . .

One more flight attendant manager asking, "How would you feel about getting your hair back to one color?"

At the initial interview, the flight attendant told the interviewer that she would settle on one color. However, like a lot of other things, once she got that uniform and those wings, it all changed! Most flight attendants are now in their sixties, seventies and nineties and are still fighting the system.

ALL THAT A FLIGHT ATTENDANT NEEDS IS ANOTHER CUT IN PAY AND . . .

Six fire trucks surrounding the day's first landing because the pilots are not sure if the landing gear is down, and eight paramedics meeting the day's second landing due to a passenger who has fainted.

And you thought that flight attendants went through six weeks of initial training just to learn how to push a beverage cart!

~

ONE MORE EXCUSE FOR A FLIGHT ATTENDANT'S BAD ATTITUDE IS . . .

Another passenger threatening your life because you have run out of chicken.

Remember when the airlines would serve a choice of complimentary beef or chicken and sometimes they would run out of your first choice? Now one pays $5 for a cookie and a bag of pretzels. Doesn't that beef sound appetizing now? What happened to those good old days?

FLIGHT ATTENDANTS DON'T NEED . . .

"Fewer" restrictions on carry-on luggage as more flight delays occur.

Who doesn't understand this? The more carry-on bags, computer bags, backpacks, diaper bags, coolers, grocery bags and Christmas gifts, the longer it takes to board these airplanes. Check the bags and don't worry about the airline losing your belongings. They can usually locate them within about two months.

ALL THAT A FLIGHT ATTENDANT NEEDS IS ANOTHER CUT IN PAY AND . . .

Another thirteen-hour delay while the airline sends the passengers to the newest five-star hotel downtown, and the crew member are sent to the cheapest hotel twenty-five miles south of the airport.

And some don't think this happens? The cheapest hotel twenty-five miles south is better than a row of seats on the aircraft or a single seat in the gate area. How does an airline ever make money?

153

JUST WHAT EVERY FLIGHT ATTENDANT NEEDS . . .

A forty-two-page instruction manual on "How to Operate A Defibrillator."

What other job requires a person, at a starting salary of $1,254 per month, to know how to operate an automated external defibrillator? Did you know that flight attendants are expected to remain on the aircraft in a smoke-filled cabin as long as they feel it is safe for them to remain on board with passengers? In a water landing they can be expected to swim through burning oil or gas. Oh yes, do not inflate the life vest until you are out of the burning area. $1,254 per month?

JUST WHAT EVERY FLIGHT ATTENDANT NEEDS . . .

Another frequent flier, seated in the emergency exit row, refusing to put down his newspaper and pay attention to the emergency safety demonstration.

Flight attendants know that frequent fliers have heard this demonstration before but have they ever watched it? In an emergency, those seated in the emergency exit row will be responsible for the safety of almost one third of the passengers on that aircraft. Either start taking this seriously, move back one row, or take the bus!

FLIGHT ATTENDANTS DON'T NEED . . .

The spouse who will not let go of the patient's hand during defibrillation.

You haven't held hands with your spouse for twenty years. Don't start now. The instructions indicate to stay away from the person during defibrillation. Just remember this moment if she lives through it!

THE LAST THING A FLIGHT ATTENDANT WANTS IS A LATE CHECK-IN AT THE AIRPORT AND . . .

An In-Flight Supervisor having a hard time believing that he accidently left his uniform apron in the dryer!

Flight attendants are not allowed many mistakes. The apron hadn't been washed for six months but now sits in the dryer at home. Aren't there really bigger issues with the flight being delayed three hours, the ice that will not be delivered to the aircraft as the ice machine is broken, one of the pilots has still not shown up and this flight is overbooked by forty passengers? Aren't there really bigger issues than no apron today?

ALL THAT A FLIGHT ATTENDANT NEEDS IS ANOTHER CUT IN PAY AND . . .

One more person who wants answers to forty-nine questions regarding the frequent flier program.

Frequent flier miles are great: no blackout dates, no limited number of seats on each flight, no restrictions, etc... until the program is three years old and the management realizes a drop in profit. Restrictions fell into place: Perhaps only two seats available on each flight for frequent fliers. And now one has to pay a fee to use those "free" frequent flier miles!

FLIGHT ATTENDANTS DON'T NEED . . .

The gate agent to present them with the unpronounceable name list of the first-class passengers.

The idea of calling a passenger by name is great, but all they really want is the wider seat and to be left alone. Gate agents, let's quit wasting the paper, ink and time on those passenger manifests and just concentrate on getting these flights out on time!

JUST WHAT EVERY FLIGHT ATTENDANT NEEDS . . .

Fifty-five children under the age of ten, all headed for Orlando, asking for "wings," though you have not see any "wings" on this aircraft for five years.

Kids just love those wings, don't they! Those are one of the nice free things left on the airplanes. The kiddies like them, and the flight attendants enjoy giving them away. Don't hesitate asking for them again, once the management reorders them!

ONE MORE EXCUSE FOR A FLIGHT ATTENDANT'S BAD ATTITUDE IS . . .

Another passenger telling them that, "Flight attendants are really a mysterious bunch, aren't they?"

Mysterious? Perhaps a bit more so than artists, musicians, beauticians and psychics! Yes, there are some different ones out there, but a few normal ones too. Most flight attendants think that they are more normal than the passengers.

THE LAST THING A FLIGHT ATTENDANT WANTS IS A LATE CHECK-IN AT THE AIRPORT AND . . .

A run-in with a flight attendant manager while wearing the scarf twisted between the belt loops rather than neatly tied around the neck as indicated in the manual.

A scarf as a belt? Creative, but flight attendants are not paid to be creative. Follow the standards set forty years ago by someone who never had to wear a uniform. Forget the fact that you are now sixty-seven years old. Just stay out of trouble!

ALL THAT A FLIGHT ATTENDANT NEEDS IS ANOTHER CUT IN PAY AND . . .

The ruling that the domestic airlines are going to allow only one free checked bag and charge $60 for each additional bag.

Could the airlines raise the ticket prices a little higher? Most people do not like fuel surcharges, baggage fees, and soda expenses. If the price of the ticket were raised, airlines may accidently show a profit. What a concept!

~~~

JUST WHAT EVERY FLIGHT ATTENDANT NEEDS . . .

No liquor seals for the beverage carts on the aircraft for the past three months.

Those flight attendants are always up to something, aren't they! Flight attendants are required to lock up the beverage carts at the end of each day. Who do you suppose is called in to talk to management when the cart is short forty-two mini liquor bottles and seventeen cans of beer? Either put enough seals on the aircraft or talk to the other employees who get onto the aircraft after the flight attendants get off.

ONE MORE EXCUSE FOR A FLIGHT ATTENDANT'S BAD ATTITUDE IS . . .

The realization that they are working on the day that the president of the United States is coming to town!

Everyone knows that this high-security situation means a two- to ten-hour delay before the scheduled departure time. Everyone knows that crew scheduling will want the entire crew to check in at the regular check-in time, "just in case!" "Industry standard" dictates that there is no pay during the delay.

FLIGHT ATTENDANTS DON'T NEED ...

The airline to announce that it plans to hire 750 new flight attendants for you to retrain once they have completed the airline's six-week training program.

The airlines provide an excellent flight attendant training program that all new hires must successfully complete prior to being certified to fly. Unfortunately, once they start flying, many established flight attendants feel they need to step in and "retrain." Though every flight attendant carries a company-issued manual of about 70,000 pages outlining how to do their job, every flight attendant has some addendums. Flight attendants, leave the training with the instructors.

ALL THAT A FLIGHT ATTENDANT NEEDS IS ANOTHER CUT IN PAY AND . . .

One more newspaper article for the already unhappy customers: "The Aviation System Is Not Working Well."

Who says "The Aviation System Is Not Working Well?" Mergers, cut backs, delays, passengers purchasing their own food, pillows, blankets and flight attendants older than water! Why complain? Many airline ticket prices are lower now than they were ten years ago.

JUST WHAT EVERY FLIGHT ATTENDANT NEEDS . . .

Another passenger who thinks he is going to get you fired.

It would take an act of God to get a crew member fired! Almost all flight attendants in this country belong to a union. The rudest and meanest flight attendant will still be flying in thirty years, so quit writing and telling management that the flight attendant never brought you another cup of tea.

THE LAST THING A FLIGHT ATTENDANT WANTS IS A LATE CHECK-IN AT THE AIRPORT AND . . .

One more passenger complaining that the airline does not have an "interline baggage agreement" with his connecting flight.

Now this means that the passenger is going to have to go down to baggage claim, pick up his fifteen pieces of checked luggage, take them all back upstairs and check them in with the next airline for his connecting flight. What a mess! May he connect with his next flight? If not, the airline will at least say, "We are sorry," or "That is unfortunate!"

JUST WHAT EVERY FLIGHT ATTENDANT NEEDS . . .

A first-time flier wanting to pay you $1.00 for his coke.

Most airlines still offer complimentary pop, but this could all change next month.

~~~

ALL THAT A FLIGHT ATTENDANT NEEDS IS ANOTHER CUT IN PAY AND . . .

One hundred passengers asking if the drinks will be complimentary due to the thirty-minute delay.

Complimentary? As a rule of thumb, complimentary only goes into effect if the delay is caused by the airline. When it is an act of God, such as the thirty-minute delay caused by a thunderstorm in Portland, the airplane cannot take off on schedule. Come on, pay for the drinks and give the airline a chance to make a nickel!

JUST WHAT EVERY FLIGHT ATTENDANT NEEDS ...

Another passenger asking, "What is the fuel tank capacity of this aircraft?"

With the current cost of fuel, one can be sure that the capacity is a lot greater than that which is actually in there! It is an unfortunate situation, but the price of the airline ticket probably doesn't cover the cost of the fuel. Isn't it time that the airline increases the price of the tickets?

FLIGHT ATTENDANTS DON'T NEED ...

The passenger seated in 7-B asking if he can try the "push button" operation of the entry door.

Please don't push any buttons on these airplane doors. It takes flight attendants six weeks of training just to learn the operation of that door, not to mention the nine tests that are given on its operation. Remember to push the toilet's "flush" button in the lavatory and the flight attendants will be very grateful!

ALL THAT A FLIGHT ATTENDANT NEEDS IS ANOTHER CUT IN PAY AND . . .

The Air Transport Association saying that major airlines have spent three billion dollars on redesigning web sites, but refuse a fifty cent hourly pay increase for its flight attendants.

At most airlines, flight attendants who have flown for twelve years or thirty-two years all make the same hourly wage and are fortunate to receive a fifty-cent-per-hour pay increase per year. But the real question is: Why isn't the turnover higher? No one quits!

FLIGHT ATTENDANTS
DON'T NEED ...

One more bulletin outlining "Service Procedures," when they know it's fares and schedules that bring passengers back.

Service procedures mean: 1) beverage service to first-class passengers while coach passengers are still boarding, 2) selling headsets, blankets and, perhaps, pillows, 3) serving a beverage to all passengers, 4) probably serving a hot meal to all passengers, 5) serving another beverage to all passengers, 6) picking up everyone's garbage, 7) more coffee to all. Isn't the bottom line really the price of the ticket and the flight schedule?

ALL THAT A FLIGHT ATTENDANT NEEDS IS ANOTHER CUT IN PAY AND . . .

One hundred and ten passengers onboard when the flight has been catered for one hundred and sixty passengers.

Way too much waste on over-catered meals, lemons, limes, printed cups and napkins, but don't pay those flight attendants another nickel. With one more pay increase, some flight attendants may no longer qualify for food stamps!

FLIGHT ATTENDANTS DON'T NEED . . .

A different set of rules for each airline.

Does one use carts in first-class or not? Just trays and never carts? Which is the best system? Whichever, flight attendants make the system work as the original system was designed by someone who had never done the job. Somewhat messed up or really messed up?

JUST WHAT EVERY FLIGHT ATTENDANT NEEDS . . .

The passenger seated in 1-D who thinks it is okay for him to stow his briefcase and coat in the bin marked "emergency equipment only."

Oh my, the FAA would be so mad if they saw a briefcase and coat on top of that megaphone and life raft. Flight attendants don't want to have to move passenger's belongings once the aircraft has landed in the middle of the ocean to remove that ninety-pound life raft, get it out of the aircraft, inflated, and into those thirteen-foot waves.

ONE MORE EXCUSE FOR A FLIGHT ATTENDANT'S BAD ATTITUDE IS . . .

A beverage cart partner, poked by another passenger to get her attention, who replies, "You are liable to be killed!"

Most flight attendants don't like to be touched or poked. Be careful, flight attendants are a part of an independent workforce. They can easily kill each other. You don't want to be next!

FLIGHT ATTENDANTS DON'T NEED . . .

An in-flight manager getting on the aircraft fifteen minutes prior to departure to "help board."

Help board? Many of these in-flight managers have never been flight attendants. It's just part of the "industry standard" to hire former managers, with fourteen years of retail management experience who have never been on an airplane, to manage 200 flight attendants! Here we go!

THE LAST THING A FLIGHT ATTENDANT WANTS IS A LATE CHECK-IN AT THE AIRPORT AND . . .

Another check-in at 3 a.m.

Flight attendants did not go to an airline for a 9 to 5 job! The closest one will ever see to a 9 to 5 job as a flight attendant may be 9 p.m. to 5 a.m. That is just part of the variety and glamour of the position. Go work for a bank if you don't like it. Everyone would like to move up one more number in seniority!

ALL THAT A FLIGHT ATTENDANT NEEDS IS ANOTHER CUT IN PAY AND . . .

One more passenger asking, "Do you like your job? Do you do this full time? What do you like about your job?"

Now they are even asking if flight attendants live in houses, their age, their marital status, their salary, and their layover schedule. The answers to these questions are: yes, in my 60s, no, about $37 per hour, no.

JUST WHAT EVERY FLIGHT ATTENDANT NEEDS . . .

Another family of four questioning why they have been assigned seats in rows eight, fifteen, twenty-two and thirty-one, when they checked in twelve minutes prior to departure.

Twelve minutes prior to departure? The gate agent only let them on because they told her that they were going to their uncle's funeral. Do you know that the airline found out that their uncle had died nine years ago? Is anyone aware of how much information the airline can learn about a person? Beware!

ONE MORE EXCUSE FOR A FLIGHT ATTENDANT'S BAD ATTITUDE IS . . .

A crisis and a defibrillator with missing pieces.

Who packed this defibrillator anyway? The pads that connect the patient to the defibrillator are not there! Do you know that flight attendants have letters from management placed into their files when empty pop cans have been left in those beverage carts? What happens to the person who packed this defibrillator?

FLIGHT ATTENDANTS DON'T NEED . . .

One more passenger seated in first-class asking during the hot towel service, "Are those tortillas?"

Either at the beginning or the end of the flight, rolled up hot towels are frequently offered to first-class passengers to clean their hands. Please don't try to eat them and don't use them to clean out your ears. Flight attendants see just about everything!

ALL THAT A FLIGHT ATTENDANT NEEDS IS ANOTHER CUT IN PAY AND . . .

The airline to implement one more "surcharge!"

Should the airlines just raise the fares and drop the surcharges? Now there is an "accommodation fee" of $7 to have the flight attendants stow passengers carry-on bags in the overhead compartment. That must come to a stop quickly! A flight attendant's medical coverage is not good!

THE LAST THING A FLIGHT
ATTENDANT WANTS IS
A LATE CHECK-IN AT
THE AIRPORT AND . . .

A passenger telling them that the baggage handlers need to smile more!

Baggage handlers, smile? I realize that one can see them from the aircraft as they are removing luggage down below, but baggage handlers are not paid to smile. How about some of those flight attendants who haven't smiled in twenty years and appear that they could kill their family!

~~~~~~~

ALL THAT A FLIGHT
ATTENDANT NEEDS IS
ANOTHER CUT IN PAY AND . . .

One more flight when the flight attendant at the back door calls to say, "We have the passenger in 27-D on oxygen!"

Oh boy. You recognize this passenger from a previous flight when he pulled this same thing. What some won't do to get a little attention!

JUST WHAT EVERY FLIGHT ATTENDANT NEEDS . . .

Another passenger asking if this airline still flies to Mazatlan while the flight attendant knows that this airline has never flown to Mazatlan!

Flight attendants often wonder if passengers are more aware of these things than flight attendants are. With the ever-changing flight schedules that airlines throw together, perhaps the airline DID go to Mazatlan thirty years ago. But the flight attendant really becomes confused when the passenger says that all three flight attendants working today's flight were working that flight to Mazatlan!

ONE MORE EXCUSE FOR A FLIGHT ATTENDANT'S BAD ATTITUDE IS . . .

A call, immediately after push back, from the flight attendants working in the back of the aircraft saying that there is no demo equipment.

D emo equipment includes the safety information card that the flight attendant is holding up at the beginning of the flight, the seat belt that is used to show the passengers how to buckle in (for those who have not been in a car lately), and finally the oxygen mask. When a set is missing, the aircraft must return to the gate to obtain this equipment. The return will result in a thirty-minute delay. It's almost a miracle that airplanes ever run on time. Do they?

ALL THAT A FLIGHT ATTENDANT NEEDS IS ANOTHER CUT IN PAY AND . . .

One more passenger asking, "How much do you make?"

Curious. Isn't that kind of like asking someone how much they weigh? A flight attendant with ten years seniority makes about $34 per hour. How much do you make?

JUST WHAT EVERY FLIGHT ATTENDANT NEEDS . . .

Another passenger asking if he can use the telephone located at the jumpseat to call his office.

This telephone is an intercom that is only connected throughout the aircraft. It is not connected to any telephone company or your office. Don't even think of getting out your cell phone to make that call. Your office will find out soon enough that you are not really sick but on your way to Hawaii for a week's vacation.

ONE MORE EXCUSE FOR A FLIGHT ATTENDANT'S BAD ATTITUDE IS . . .

A navy blue uniform required for landing in 119-degree weather in Palm Springs.

Sounds practical to me! Passengers are comfortably dressed for 119-degree weather, but flight attendants are wearing navy blue. It is about the only way to get respect from the passengers. Casual attire would make the passengers think that flight attendants were on their way to a car wash.

FLIGHT ATTENDANT'S DON'T NEED . . .

One more drug-addict-looking guy from Santa Cruz, California, exiting the lavatory and belligerently denying the smoke behind him.

Flight attendants are real tired of having the police meet the California and New York flights because of illegal behavior in those lavatories. Some flight attendants should have been law enforcement officers. Watch out, maybe they have been!

THE LAST THING A FLIGHT ATTENDANT WANTS IS A LATE CHECK-IN AT THE AIRPORT AND . . .

Two passengers asking, "Why can't we get off the airplane?" while being served a hot breakfast during a two-hour ground delay at the gate.

The gate agents don't want to see 149 passengers back in their space, so they feed the passengers in hopes that they will all go to sleep and forget about the delay. In reality, the agents are afraid that the passengers will drift out of the immediate area and miss their flight when it actually leaves. Guess what, only four or five will drift away and if they do, there is another flight leaving soon.

ALL THAT A FLIGHT ATTENDANT NEEDS IS ANOTHER CUT IN PAY AND . . .

The flight attendant manager meeting you at check-in before a four-day trip to measure the height of your heels, the length of your hair, and the size of your earrings.

It doesn't matter if you have flown for 10 months or 110 years, most flight attendants are treated like children. Flight attendants are not allowed to wear their uniform sweater when walking through the airport terminal without the uniform blazer over it! Did you know that?

JUST WHAT EVERY FLIGHT ATTENDANT NEEDS ...

The realization that payroll has been paying a $2.00 per hour increase for the past three months, while the union contract increase was really only to be ninety-seven cents per hour.

Now you owe the company $310.03 and, without warning, it is all deducted from the next paycheck. The IRS even offers a payment plan, doesn't it?

FLIGHT ATTENDANTS DON'T NEED ...

Another passenger who has had way too much to drink asking, "Can I say something on that PA?"

Don't ever act like you have had too much to drink on an airplane! The next thing you will hear over the PA will be that the aircraft has made an emergency landing and that the local police will be coming on board the aircraft to remove the passenger.

ONE MORE EXCUSE FOR A FLIGHT ATTENDANT'S BAD ATTITUDE IS . . .

Another passenger refusing to remove his headphones while trying to find out what he would like to drink.

Flight attendants, try this: Place the napkin in front of the passenger wearing the headphones, wait until the headphones are removed, then ask if they would like a beverage. It's pretty simple and you will not have to repeat yourself. Passengers, how about removing the headphones when you see the napkin headed in your direction!

JUST WHAT EVERY FLIGHT ATTENDANT NEEDS . . .

Another nervous passenger asking, "How long will I have to wait for my rental car in Boston?"

This flight is running four hours late! We are arriving in Boston at 3 a.m. and the car rentals open around 8 a.m. Five hours! Also remember, this is a weather delay and not a mechanical delay caused by the airline, so the hotel will have to be at your expense.

ONE MORE EXCUSE FOR A FLIGHT ATTENDANT'S BAD ATTITUDE IS . . .

To be stuck in the personnel lift on the wide-body aircraft with the heaviest flight attendant in the industry!

The elevator measures only about twenty-six inches by thirty-six inches. When was the last time you saw a flight attendant that small?

THE LAST THING A FLIGHT ATTENDANT WANTS IS A LATE CHECK-IN AT THE AIRPORT AND . . .

Another thirty-five-minute delay due to thirty-seven "gate-checked bags."

T hese are bags that passengers have gotten past the gate agent and brought onto the aircraft to avoid checking. Most flight attendants are quick to see that the four-foot by nine-foot box is too large for the overhead bins. If an on-time departure is really that important, check those bags. Delays would drop drastically!

ALL THAT A FLIGHT ATTENDANT NEEDS IS ANOTHER CUT IN PAY AND . . .

The airline to implement one more "surcharge!"

S houldn't airlines just raise the fares and drop the surcharges? One airline is charging passengers to use the air vents located in the panel above their seats. With the acceptance of a major credit card, the unit will provide circulating air for thirty minutes!

FLIGHT ATTENDANTS
DON'T NEED . . .

Another newspaper article stating, "Local airport currently accommodating forty-eight flights per hour, but was constructed to accommodate thirty-six!"

Any wonder why the delays? Perhaps the airports that were constructed to accommodate thirty-six aircraft per hour should cut back to twenty. Wouldn't that keep them on schedule, keep both the passengers and flight attendants in a better mood, and reduce the staff in the airline complaint department? Why not just build another airport across town like they did in Chicago!

JUST WHAT EVERY FLIGHT ATTENDANT NEEDS ...

One attentive passenger asking, "If there are eight doors on this aircraft, why do you use just one for boarding?"

This question provides some insight about the industry's common sense. Eight doors, and most airlines use only one. I guess they like to see passengers who are over ninety years old walk the narrow aisle to row thirty-seven.

ALL THAT A FLIGHT ATTENDANT NEEDS IS ANOTHER CUT IN PAY AND ...

Another newspaper headline stating, "Brought Back to Life at 29,000 Feet."

Flight attendants can save lives. They can assist with sinus discomfort, shock, seizures, hypothermia, and even childbirth. Let's see, regarding childbirth, these aisles are only about eighteen inches wide, the galley floors are dirty, and we don't have any free blankets. Not an easy assist on that one.

ONE MORE EXCUSE FOR A FLIGHT ATTENDANT'S BAD ATTITUDE IS . . .

Another international flight requiring customs forms for 140 passengers, although with all of the mistakes, flight attendants really need 240 forms.

This is the form required prior to entering countries such as Mexico and Japan. As long as one is going to a foreign country, please bring a pen along. Read before you write. The flight number is not August 8, the city you are entering is not M901447181211-6 (your passport number) and your birthplace is not Bill (your first name). Does all of this really matter? Are those customs agents really reading any of this?

FLIGHT ATTENDANTS DON'T NEED . . .

Fellow flight attendants acting like lead flight attendants if they're not.

If a flight attendant has been flying for twenty-one years and chooses not to take the lead position for that trip, quit telling the person with one year of seniority how to do the job. A flight attendant can increase his/her income by about $4,000 per year just by taking lead. Why doesn't someone with twenty-one years of seniority take the lead position anyway?

ALL THAT A FLIGHT ATTENDANT NEEDS IS ANOTHER CUT IN PAY AND . . .

A one-hour "pretzel flight" with another passenger asking, "Is this all that we get?"

You, the passenger, only paid $79 for the flight. The pretzels are free and so is the pop. Next time, bring a sandwich, an apple and a candy bar from home. You will probably feel better for it and not get food poisoning.

PAYING PASSENGERS
REALLY DON'T WANT . . .

Another tired flight attendant telling them that they "cannot" fit their sixty-eight inch carry-on bag underneath their seat!

F olks, the space under those seats measures about eleven inches high and sixteen inches wide. The sixty-eight inch carry-on is just not going to come close! Do you know that more flights could leave on time if there were fewer carry-on bags and more checked bags? I guess that the airline will just get you there when it gets you there. Oh, we do anyway, don't we!

FLIGHT ATTTENDANTS DON'T NEED . . .

Another passenger looking into the cockpit while boarding and saying, "I hope they all got a good night's sleep."

Pilots and flight attendants have what is called "minimum crew rest" and all of them take advantage of that. Do you know that the best thing one can do for the flight attendants is to fall asleep? Oh, and when they come through with the beverage and meal carts, please don't wake up the person next to you. Sometimes rest is more important than food.

ALL THAT A FLIGHT ATTENDANT NEEDS IS ANOTHER CUT IN PAY AND . . .

The newspaper headline: "Airlines Under Pressure to Provide Medical Care."

A salary of $1,254 per month and expected to do more than pour pop? I wonder if that is why so many flight attendants have chosen to become full-time nurses and only part-time flight attendants. Flight attendants aren't stupid! Just ask them!

JUST WHAT EVERY FLIGHT ATTENDANT NEEDS . . .

An obligation to tell the airline that they are so flexible that they will be happy to be based in Portland, Philadelphia, Phoenix, or Pensacola.

Newly hired flight attendants will tell the company anything because they really want the job that much. If they even mentioned that they were not willing to relocate, they would never be given a second interview. For $1,254 per month, why not relocate?

ONE MORE EXCUSE FOR A FLIGHT ATTENDANT'S BAD ATTITUDE IS . . .

Sixty-five passengers asking, "What is this flight number?" when they are trying to complete their international paperwork.

That's okay, not everyone has flown before. All one has to do is listen. The agent at the ticket counter tells all passengers the flight number at least two times and writes it on the boarding envelope. Then the gate agent announces the flight number about seventy-nine times in the gate area. The lead flight attendant announces it about four times during the boarding process. The flight number is written on the boarding pass. Next time you fly, keep the boarding pass handy and don't make this too difficult on yourself. Total number of times that the flight number was announced: 85!

FLIGHT ATTENDANTS
DON'T NEED . . .

Ten more passengers standing up to get their valuables out of the overhead bins before the aircraft comes to a complete stop at the gate.

Remember, the seat belt sign applies to everyone, regardless of the number of miles flown. Hint: If you can see the flight attendants in their jumpseats, remain seated as long as they are still seated because they are not going to get up until that sign has been turned off. This hint mainly applies to passengers with more than seventy million flight miles.

JUST WHAT EVERY FLIGHT ATTENDANT NEEDS . . .

Seven out of the eight flight attendants working together think that the article in the in-flight magazine entitled "Cosmetic Surgery" was written for them!

Flight attendants are usually a pretty good-looking group, aren't they? It doesn't come without a high price, however. How much of their sick time is devoted to cosmetic surgery rather than all of those claimed-to-be-back-surgeries from the beverage carts?

PAYING PASSENGERS REALLY DON'T WANT . . .

Weather delays occurring every time that they fly "your" airline!

Airlines control a lot of things but probably not the weather. But don't hesitate asking the airline for a free upgrade to first class or even a free ticket due to that twenty-seven-minute weather delay. Don't hesitate asking, but every airline will turn you down for these acts of God.

ONE MORE EXCUSE FOR A FLIGHT ATTENDANT'S BAD ATTITUDE IS . . .

A seniority of only nine years and faced with all five-day trips for the next ten years!

Remember when you told them in your interview that you would relocate anywhere, that you enjoyed variety in your work and that you didn't mind working weekends? Well, now you are based in Cleveland, and the variety in this job consists of which side of the cart you will place the cups and juice on today. You haven't seen a weekend off since you started and probably won't for another ten years! Isn't it amazing that airlines can receive 100 applications each day for this career? Career?

FLIGHT ATTTENDANTS DON'T NEED . . .

One more frequent flier who thinks that everything can be justified by the number of miles they have flown.

Frequent fliers are a great asset to any airline, but they have not purchased enough tickets to qualify them as owner of the airline. Set a good example for others who have not flown as often. It's all small stuff, such as staying seated until the seat belt sign has been turned off and turning off your cell phone when the announcement is made.

FLIGHT ATTENDANTS DON'T NEED . . .

One more passenger who thinks he is too good to be seated in "coach," even though that is where he is always seated!

It is what it is. Too good to be seated in coach? Let loose with that upgrade charge for first class next time. Your personality would probably fit better in first class. The question is, can you afford it?

JUST WHAT EVERY FLIGHT
ATTENDANT NEEDS . . .

An eighteen-year-old passenger, listening to the audio system, asking, "Is this all there is?" although there are ten other channels listed for the in-flight audio system.

U nfortunately, this is all there is! Flight attendants can request that the audio channels be updated, but this may not occur within the next ten years. Meantime, perhaps the teenager could purchase an iPod or DVD player for their next flight. We certainly look forward to welcoming him aboard another one of our flights before he is twenty-eight!

ALL THAT A FLIGHT ATTENDANT NEEDS IS ANOTHER CUT IN PAY AND . . .

One more passenger wanting to know, "How many passengers are on here today?"

Passengers have a lot of questions. Are they concerned because they heard the gate agent say that there are 212 checked bags on this flight and that this aircraft has had five coats of paint? Bags and paint are heavy, very heavy. This aircraft has 148 seats, there are four vacant seats, so there must be 144 passengers.

ONE MORE EXCUSE FOR A FLIGHT ATTENDANT'S BAD ATTITUDE IS . . .

Two of the "weakest links" in the flight attendant industry are working together on the same schedule for the entire month.

This really is a job where team work is important. Instead you get two lazy flight attendants working together, doing the minimum required, and one thinking about using some of their sick time! Better take a look at how much sick time you can use.

FLIGHT ATTENDANTS DON'T NEED . . .

Another passenger telling them that they are a "gold" card holder.

O nce again, whether you are a red, green, blue or gold card holder, all of the rules still apply. The airlines appreciate the business, but flight attendants don't appreciate it when passengers make up their own rules. Please, either put the newspaper down, fall asleep, or pay attention to the announcements.

~~~~~~~

ALL THAT A FLIGHT ATTENDANT NEEDS IS ANOTHER CUT IN PAY AND . . .

The airline to implement one more "surcharge!"

S houldn't airlines just raise the fares and drop the surcharges? Has anyone heard that an airline up north is talking about a surcharge to use the lavatory? Isn't this stupid! Stupid, stupid, stupid! Could one use cash or is only a credit card acceptable? Would there be a flat charge or would it be based on length of time occupied? Stupid, stupid, stupid!

JUST WHAT EVERY FLIGHT ATTENDANT NEEDS . . .

Three subway transfers just to get from home to the aircraft parked at New York's La Guardia Airport.

Flight attendants will do anything for this job, won't they! They have to leave home by 5 a.m. to check in for a noon flight at La Guardia. Some even commute from Los Angeles, Dallas and Memphis to check in at their base in New York! Wouldn't you rather just stay at home and work for the local bank?

JUST WHAT EVERY FLIGHT ATTENDANT NEEDS . . .

To read about "N-I-M-B-Y" pertaining to airports!

No one wants more new runways in their neighborhood. Well, a new runway or longer delays at the airport? Many say, "Not In My Back Yard!" Too late. The airport was there first!

ALL THAT A FLIGHT ATTENDANT NEEDS IS ANOTHER CUT IN PAY AND . . .

A recycling program with few rewards!

Flight attendants, go ahead and recycle those millions of pop cans into garbage bags that leak, which will be taken to a recycling center. Do this daily! Many flight attendants end up in the emergency room with cuts from removing those tops. Just something more for the flight attendants to do!

ONE MORE EXCUSE FOR A FLIGHT ATTENDANT'S BAD ATTITUDE IS . . .

The discovery–at 4 a.m.–that there isn't any hot water in the hotel, prior to their fourteen-hour work day.

Aircraft water lines tend to freeze in the winter. Does this happen in hotels, too? Do hotels have only one water heater? Oh well, clean up with the cold rusty water in the hotel and get down to the lobby for the 5 a.m. check-in. No wonder some flight attendants are so crabby before they even get to the airplane.

ONE MORE EXCUSE FOR A FLIGHT ATTENDANT'S BAD ATTITUDE IS . . .

Wondering where all of this luggage is coming from while luggage manufacturers are complaining that sales are off 15%.

Who thought it was a good idea to make a "rolling bag" out of a five-foot by seven-foot crate? Too large for the bins! These "rolling bags" have gotten so large that now the wheels turn sideways so that the bag will fit down the aisle. Still way too large for the bins! What about this: If it has wheels, it has to be checked. Good idea?

FLIGHT ATTENDANTS
DON'T NEED . . .

That airline route map, illustrated in the in-flight magazine, that has not been updated for three years.

Shouldn't those maps be kept up to date? No wonder the flight attendants don't know if the airline still flies to Denver or Mazatlan! Both are still on the route map, but they discontinued flying to Denver five years ago, and no one really knows if they have ever gone to the other.

ALL THAT A FLIGHT ATTENDANT NEEDS IS ANOTHER CUT IN PAY AND . . .

The discovery that their big paycheck for the month is short $12.00 again.

No one seems to know why this happens. Scheduling is not responsible and payroll certainly is not. The company probably will not cut a special check for a flight attendant unless the check is short $7,000 or more. You will simply have to wait until the next pay period. But it may not be there then! Where is that $12.00?

JUST WHAT EVERY FLIGHT ATTENDANT NEEDS . . .

One more pilot with a picture of Mickey Mouse, Goofy or even the president of the airline covering his picture on his company-issued ID!

Oh my, those pilots certainly can be creative, can't they! The pictures on the IDs are not the greatest, but isn't it just a pass to get you onto the airplane? Flight attendants don't even think about doing this. Aren't those pilots given a lot of credit though!

ALL THAT A FLIGHT
ATTENDANT NEEDS IS
ANOTHER CUT IN PAY AND . . .

The passenger who has not cleaned her own house in five years insisting that the flight attendant get a hot towel to sanitize her tray table!

Sure, flight attendants will clean off a passenger's tray table, but do you have any idea of the number of children that use magic markers on them? Parents, do you really allow your children to write on your furniture at home, the home that hasn't been cleaned in five years? Please bring some paper to go along with those markers or leave the markers at home.

PAYING PASSENGERS
REALLY DON'T WANT ...

Another newspaper article stating that one more flight will be added at the local airport that already has delays every day at the same time.

Adding one more flight at one more airport will probably delay seventeen more flights within the next two hours. Schedulers, can you just review this, one more time? How much planning goes into these decisions? Any?

FLIGHT ATTENDANTS
DON'T NEED . . .

Another 100% oxford nylon hotel shower curtain, made in Mexico with U.S. materials, wrapping around them in the shower after a 16-hour day!

The hotels, just another glamorous part of this career! The airline normally books flight attendants in fairly nice hotels, some nicer than others. Why do flight attendants often check into the hotel just when "happy hour" has ended? Why are they often assigned rooms that are already occupied? Why are the "crew rooms" always at the end of the hall, two miles from the elevator? Haven't they walked about ninety miles in the aisle of that aircraft! Oh, hotel, please remove that oxford nylon shower curtain and replace it with a nice shower door.

ALL THAT A FLIGHT ATTENDANT NEEDS IS ANOTHER CUT IN PAY AND . . .

A notice that payroll has now deducted $822 for the $750 uniform.

Everyone makes mistakes, right? The company has just deducted $72 more from the paycheck than they should have, but the flight attendant will probably not be reimbursed within the next six years! And yet flight attendants can't make mistakes! Show up one time without your scarf, tie or wings and you won't hear the end of it. Perhaps flight attendants aren't human. We know many of them are not normal!

JUST WHAT EVERY FLIGHT ATTENDANT NEEDS . . .

When doing the emergency safety demonstration he notices that the new mother seated in 3-C is staring at him while sucking on her infant's pacifier!

This looks gross! Flight attendants see almost everything on these airplanes and this is one of the worst. Not cute, practical, maybe, but not cute. Please don't ask the flight attendant to hold it either. Well, some would rather hold the pacifiers than dirty diapers. Neither, please!

ONE MORE EXCUSE FOR A FLIGHT ATTENDANT'S BAD ATTITUDE IS . . .

Another bottle of "Lav Spray" to freshen up one more galley cupboard!

They smell like new from the manufacturer for about one week. The galley kitchens are usually right next to the lavatories. Wouldn't it be a better design to place the lavatories elsewhere? Your kitchen doesn't smell like a lavatory because it is probably twenty or thirty feet away from the kitchen. Manufacturers, please try splitting these galleys and lavatories.

FLIGHT ATTENDANTS DON'T NEED . . .

One more 369-pound passenger telling them that his tray table is broken.

Folks, it is not the tray table! Try first class next time. You will be a lot more comfortable and so will the flight attendants serving you.

ALL THAT A FLIGHT ATTENDANT NEEDS IS ANOTHER CUT IN PAY AND . . .

A co-worker who thinks there is a better job someplace else.

Although some flight attendants think there really is a better job elsewhere, they have performed this one for thirty-seven years or more. Where else could one go to work and see 750 smiling faces every day, be on duty from 4 a.m. until 9 p.m., and get into trouble with a manager when one forgets to get another cocktail for the passenger seated in row 19. Many flight attendants are in their sixties, seventies and nineties and are still being called into a manager's office. Very little trust is given to flight attendants, but that is okay. If you really don't like it, get out. I would like to move up one more number in seniority!

JUST WHAT EVERY FLIGHT ATTENDANT NEEDS . . .

After the announcement, "All of your carry-on items must be stowed in the overhead bins or under the seat in front of you," the new mother places her infant car seat in the overhead bin with her infant still in it!

Flight attendants don't ever want to see this! Those bins get so dark when the doors are closed on them!

PAYING PASSENGERS REALLY DON'T WANT . . .

Another flight attendant telling them that the seat belt sign "is on for their safety!"

Many passengers need to go to the restroom or stand up in the aisle just as the seat belt sign is illuminated. When nature calls, what is one to do? Flight attendants seem to use the restrooms at their convenience and not many of them end up on the ceiling of the aircraft. Remain seated and don't take a chance!

FLIGHT ATTENDANTS
DON'T NEED . . .

Another reservation sales agent promising a child's meal and a vegetarian meal on the flight that has only served pretzels, cookies and crackers for the past five years.

Aren't these computers just great! Agents sometimes offer special meals on flights that don't even serve meals! Oh, I guess that now they do call pretzels, cookies and crackers a meal! That is "industry standard." Bring your own meal, we will supply the beverage, and then you are sure to enjoy the flight!

ALL THAT A FLIGHT ATTENDANT NEEDS IS ANOTHER CUT IN PAY AND . . .

One more passenger asking where they should eat, sleep and drink once they arrive in San Francisco!

G uess what, this airline attendant has already been flying for fourteen days this month and she did not even know we were headed for San Francisco! When in doubt, ask the gate agents when you get off the airplane in San Francisco. They live there!

JUST WHAT EVERY FLIGHT ATTENDANT NEEDS . . .

To notice that, ten minutes after the announcement "portable electronic devices must be turned off and stowed," the passenger seated in 26-C still has his computer on.

These computers, electronic devices, cell phones, DVD players, etc. have become a real headache for every flight attendant today. One would see a drastic improvement in flight attendant morale if the airline would require that all electronic devices be turned off BEFORE entering the jetway to board the aircraft.

FLIGHT ATTENDANTS
DON'T NEED . . .

One more passenger reading in the in-flight magazine that the "baggage liability limit" is only $2,500 in the event that his checked bag with a value of $4,700 is lost.

Passengers wonder everyday, "Why did I have to check that bag?" Well, because it would not come close to fitting into an overhead bin plus it weights 500 pounds. So, you just checked a bag with a contents value of $4,700 and if you never see it again the airline will pay you up to $2,500 but probably more like $990 after depreciation of the contents. Oh, and airline employees, no coverage at all for your checked bag. But you probably knew that!

ALL THAT A FLIGHT ATTENDANT NEEDS IS ANOTHER CUT IN PAY AND . . .

To take the lead position only to learn that the flight is booked with sixteen upgraded passengers in first class and only a total of nine passengers in coach!

Why didn't the flight attendant choose to work in coach? It must be the $3.59 per hour extra lead pay. Won't it be nice when the airlines go back to allowing only two upgraded passengers per flight? Perhaps after the airline loses another $15 million this will change. Oh, I guess it already has changed; now one "pays" about $100 to use those "free" miles.

JUST WHAT EVERY FLIGHT ATTENDANT NEEDS . . .

Another newspaper article stating, "First Class Travelers Get a Bad Rap."

Is It Today's Crass Customers or Is First Class Really Not What It Used to Be? You decide!

FLIGHT ATTENDANTS
DON'T NEED . . .

A passenger traveling from Los Angeles to Indianapolis asking. "What state will we be over when it gets dark?"

First of all, most flight attendants don't usually look out the window. They're too busy. Some may even say that they are fifty miles north of Alaska just to tell the passenger something! Just be direct and ask, "Once it gets dark, will you kindly ask the pilot to make an announcement as to our current location?" Flight attendants hate to say that they don't know something!

ALL THAT A FLIGHT ATTENDANT NEEDS IS ANOTHER CUT IN PAY AND . . .

Another in-flight magazine that explains how much the airline is "committed to and loves its passengers."

Let's see, "loves" its passengers: longer lines, more seats, less leg room and about the only thing that is free is water! If all of the airlines would just raise their fares they could bring back two more employees to make for shorter lines, remove six seats or maybe even two rows for the aircraft, and stop charging the passenger for everything on board? How are these "industry standards" working for the industry?

JUST WHAT EVERY FLIGHT ATTENDANT NEEDS . . .

One more passenger on a flight from Chicago to Seattle asking for a cup of coffee with three creams and nine sugars.

This is way too much! Thirty-seven choices of beverages including regular coffee, decaf coffee and tea. Some want it black, some want it with just cream, others want decaf with sugar and some want hot tea with lemon. Would it work better if the airline provided the coffee, decaf and tea, and the passengers brought their own cream, sugar, fake sugar, and lemon? The airline could probably even lower the fares!

ONE MORE EXCUSE FOR A FLIGHT ATTENDANT'S BAD ATTITUDE IS . . .

Their rolling suitcase, which was issued by the airline and guaranteed for another five years, falls apart in the middle of the San Diego airport.

Any idea how much flight attendants spend on luggage repairs each year? Millions! Are there any good luggage manufactures out there? We don't see any of those children's bags with the cartoon characters falling apart. Let's spend our money on those next time!

PAYING PASSENGERS
REALLY DON'T WANT . . .

To hear on the news that the local airline only does a thorough scrubbing of each lavatory trash bin every twenty-nine days!

Avoid using the lavatories on an aircraft if possible. They are very small, they smell, and they just don't come from the manufacturer very clean even when they are new! Use the public airport lavatories prior to boarding an aircraft. Don't use aircraft lavatories, and don't think too much about them, either.

ALL THAT A FLIGHT
ATTENDANT NEEDS IS
ANOTHER CUT IN PAY AND . . .

One more passenger asking, "Due to this misconnection, does the airline owe me a meal or a hotel room?"

Misconnection? A meal? The airline just gave you two first-class meals and two pieces of cheesecake. A hotel room? There isn't a hotel within sixty miles of this little airport. The next flight leaves in five hours. But remember, the airlines "love" their passengers!

JUST WHAT EVERY FLIGHT ATTENDANT NEEDS . . .

Another passenger insisting on "carrying" her rolling bag down to row twenty-five thinking that the bag is wider than she is!

Not close. It's the hips hitting the arm rests of seats "C" and "D," not the bag. Agents, how about row five next time or suggesting an upgrade to first class. Now the bag doesn't fit into the overhead bin at row twenty-five. Any wonder why airlines have delayed flights!

FLIGHT ATTENDANTS
DON'T NEED . . .

Another 10 p.m. news flash that an airline put a six-year-old "unaccompanied minor" on their flight to San Juan instead of San Jose, California.

The child arrived in San Jose twenty-four hours later, and the airline referred to it as an "unfortunate incident!" This happens a little too often, don't you think? We all make mistakes but the first mistake here was the absence of the parents. The airlines have a pretty efficient system for "unaccompanied minors" but perhaps it is not perfect. Don't worry, give it another try next year. This was just an "unfortunate incident!"

THE LAST THING A FLIGHT ATTENDANT WANTS IS A LATE CHECK-IN AT THE AIRPORT AND . . .

A passenger entering the galley asking for the address of the "Unclaimed Baggage Center" in Alabama as she wants to see if any of her things ended up there from the last time her bag was lost.

Have you ever seen this place? It is nicer than any used-clothing store one has ever seen! All of the labels have been removed, diamonds may have been replaced with cubic zirconia, but everything is very nicely displayed. Buy an airline ticket sometime and go down there. You will probably find your bag, and you can buy it back!

FLIGHT ATTENDANTS DON'T NEED . . .

One more "mini" of vodka to wash their hands as there are already nine passengers in line waiting to use the aircraft lavatory.

This is easy: Too many passengers consuming too much food and beverage with access to not enough lavatories. We need to keep the passengers, so let's get rid of the food and beverage. How about a cup of ice!

ALL THAT A FLIGHT ATTENDANT NEEDS IS ANOTHER CUT IN PAY AND . . .

The ability to afford a good moisturizer to get them through another winter.

The airplanes are so drying, a good moisturizer is so expensive, and if a flight attendant is lucky she receives a pay increase of about forty-seven cents per hour each year. Not enough to afford much moisturizer! Do you wonder why some flight attendants look the way they do?

MEATLOAF TO MAUI

"Good evening ladies and gentlemen and welcome aboard flight 1449 with non-stop service to Maui. My name is Gregg, and I will be the lead flight attendant this evening. Working from front to back are Garrett, Chloé and Tucker. Will you please direct your attention to the flight attendants as we review some of the important safety features of this aircraft."

Now, just one minute here; "good evening," it is 11 p.m., shouldn't these people be home and in bed? And, "ladies and gentlemen," oh well, is that really appropriate for everyone that has just boarded? Non-stop service, does anyone really believe that this is going to be non-stop from Chicago to Maui? Now we are into the important safety features of the aircraft, and oh boy, do the number of miles flown dictate weather you pay attention to this DEMO, as we refer to it? The passenger that flies every week is asleep. The one that flies once each month is reading the newspaper and would never allow his eyes to glance up. The passenger that flies twice a year appears somewhat interested, however, makes a point to let you know that he knows how to operate that overwing window exit! The first time flier is glued to your every move and is scared to death. Didn't they know that this thing was going to leave the ground and go over some water? That's ok, not every-one has flown before.

Meanwhile, "this aircraft has four door exits." While we point them out, some are sleeping, some reading and other's heads are spinning as those are the pas-sengers who thought the door they came through was the only one on this 139 foot aircraft. "These doors are equipped with inflatable slides." In just a matter of moments someone is going to ask you if they can try one of the slides. This is not an amusement park! "Our cabin is pressurized for your comfort, but should there be a loss of pressure, an oxygen mask will drop from the panel located directly above you." Now, you know that during the first beverage service the guy in 14-C is going to point to that panel and ask you, "what is in here?" That's ok, not everyone has flown before.

"Seat belts must be fastened when the sign is illuminat-ed." Is this really directed to those that have not been in a car recently?

By the time we point out the life vests and seat cushions (you know those seats are 17 X 18 inches) and they don't fit every passenger, the passenger that was reading the newspaper is now sleeping.

"Federal Regulations require passengers to comply with all lighted passenger signs, posted placards, etc. etc.

etc." Well, most passengers do not feel that these signs apply to them but they DO apply to everyone else!

Oh, the life rafts. "One life raft is located in a marked overhead bin in the center of the cabin, etc. etc. etc." Now, you know that the guy in 17-B is going to ask if he can pull the raft down to look at it and the guy across the aisle will ask, "are we going over that much water between Chicago and Maui?" That's ok, not everyone has flown before.

"This is a non-smoking flight, and once again federal regulations do not permit smoking in the cabin or the lavatories. Do not tamper with or destroy lavatory smoke detectors as this is also a violation of federal regulations." By now we are getting in line for take off and 2 passengers are asking if they can step outside to smoke!

"The cabin lights will be turned off for departure. Individual controls for reading lights are located in the panel located directly above you." Remember, next to the oxygen mask that 14-C did not understand? Now, you know who accidently turns on the flight attendant '1 light because that button is located right next to the ~g light button, 14-C ! Oh, along with 29-D, 21-A, ' 6-F !

"Flight time this evening is 8 hours and 20 minutes. Once we reach a comfortable cruising altitude, we will be serving you beverages, an optional hot meal, and 1 hour prior to landing in Maui, additional water and coffee."

Our turn for take off and there we are, 32,000 feet in the air, the seat belt sign is still on and now the passenger from 6-F is up at the forward lavatory saying she just can't wait any longer. Oh, what does an anurizim feel like? Ok, stay in there until the seat belt sign goes off . . . you know that it will be on for at least 15 more minutes! Now, every 3 minutes another passenger rings that flight attendant call button to ask for a pillow, a blanket, a magazine, a glass of water or to ask, "when can I use the restroom?" Oh boy, why can't they just bring their own pillow, blanket, magazine and glass of water? I know, they paid for the seat, now they own the airline!

Here is the dreaded announcement, "Ladies and Gentlemen, the captain has turned off the seat belt sign, you are free to move about the cabin. However, we suggest that you keep your seat belts comfortably fastened while you are seated." Before you can even get that said, 9 people are in line waiting to use 2 lavatories. Can they just have 1 less coffee or 1 less beer while waiting in the terminal?

Now we are going to give them more reason to use the lavatories. "At this time we will begin our first beverage service." Little do they know that we will be doing 4 beverage services during this flight. "On the carts today we have pop, pop and more pop, juice, juice and more juice, water, and guess what, more coffee! Beer, wine and cocktails are $5, the correct change is greatly appreciated." Do you have any idea how many $100 bills that we receive for one $5 can of beer? Guess what, we don't carry any change. Well, before giving out a free can of beer, we will find the $95 change! "Following the first beverage service, we will be serving you meatloaf along with a fruit cup and carrot cake available for $9."

Here we are in the aisle with the 250-pound beverage carts:

— Do you have Pepsi? No, unfortunately we only carry Coke products.

— Do you have grape juice? No, unfortunately we only have apple, orange, tomato and grapefruit.

— Do you have ice tea? No, however, we do have ice and we do have tea!

— Is it too late to order a vegetarian meal? It is always too late because unfortunately, we do not carry them.

— I would like a Pepsi with only 2 ice cubes. Do you know how many people tell us how many ice cubes to put into their cup?

— Can you move the cart so that my child can go to the bathroom? Oh, sure!

— Do you have cappachino? No, however, we have regular coffee and decaf coffee. Ok, do you have Equal? No, unfortunately we just have Sweet and Low. Ok, I will have water. As you are handing him a glass of water with about 7 ice cubes in it, what does he say . . . I don't want any ice!

— How soon will you be serving the meal? As soon as we are finished with the first beverage service. Is it served with a salad or chips? No, it is meatloaf served with a fruit cup and carrot cake.

You are finally finished with the first beverage service, and you and the cart are headed back to the galley to begin the meal service. On the way, you are stopped by 17 passengers asking for move beverages. Are these people just used to "the other" airlines that just go through one time? We will be back with this same cart 3 more times! That's ok, not everyone has flown before!

Getting that cart back into the galley is quite an ordeal as 11 passengers are now waiting to use the lavatories.

Oh boy, now you get a call from the flight attendants in the back galley and guess what, they forgot to turn the ovens on. Oh well, these meals take 19 minutes. Just give us a call when you are ready. It is an 8 hour and 20 minute flight—is there any rush? Well, many flight attendants think so because they want to get those lights turned off and put the passengers to sleep. Ask a flight attendant sometime what they like best about this job and many of them will say when the passengers fall asleep! Did they tell that to the interviewer when they were originally hired?

The flight attendants call from the back to report that one oven is empty. We are now short about 24 meals! No problem, we will be on the ground in less than 7 hours! Just be quiet with the carts, try not to wake those that are sleeping and this will 'probably' work! Here come the meal and beverage carts into the aisle all at one time. Turn the lights down. Perhaps no one will wake up!

Within the first 3 rows:

— Do you have a vegetarian meal? Unfortunately, we only have meatloaf tonight.

— Do you have Kosher meals? Unfortunately, we only have meatloaf tonight.

— Do you have a seafood meal? Unfortunately we only have meatloaf tonight.

— Do you have just a cup of soup? Unfortunately . . .

Get it? We are going to have meals left over; plenty of extra meals.

Well, we made it through and actually have 17 extra meals. More beverages and more ice and more beverages and more ice and more for the garbage pick up. You know it as a race to get those garbage carts into the aisle before there are 19 more passengers in line for those lavatories!

Oh, we aren't finished yet. Now, another coffee service! In one hand we have a tray of cups, cream, sugar and stir sticks and in the other hand, the coffee pot. On this trip down the aisle the couple in row 4 asks if you have tea there! No, unfortunately this is just coffee. Would you like me to bring you some tea? Yes, that would be nice. The lady in 4-C asks, do you have Coke there? No, unfortunately this is just coffee. Would you like me to bring you some Coke? Yes, that would be good. The guy in 7-A asks is that Club Soda? No, unfortunately this is just coffee. Would you like me to bring you some Club Soda? Ya, with lime too. Now, I dread approaching row 14 but here I am. 14-C immediately asks, do you have Bloody Mary Mix there? No, however, I will bring some to you right away!

That completes our beverage and meal and beverage and garbage and coffee service for now. Oh, except for tea for row 4, Coke for row 4, Club Soda for row 7, and Bloody Mary Mix for you know who! It just seems that there is always a 14-C on every flight!

The flight attendants will "monitor" the aisle every 10–12 minutes for the next 5 hours before they do the next beverage and snack service. Remember, flight attendants, no knitting on the jumpseats, no crossword puzzles, no magazines, no newspapers, no nails polished, no letter writing, and no rug hooking. Review your manuals, or socialize with the passengers and try to keep them awake!

Oh, here we go! Here comes 14-C with his Bloody Mary Mix glass and lots of questions:

— Do you fly this route every week?

— How long have you been doing this?

— I am captain Jones's neighbor; do you know him?

— How much do they pay you here?

That's ok, not everyone has flow before!

~~~~~~

Remember 4-C with the Coke? Here she comes:

— Were you on our flight to Orlando about 3 years ago?

— Have you gained weight and lost some hair since we last saw you?

— How did you get that fried chicken? I brought it from home. You know, I want to keep up my weight.

Oh, here comes the guy from 7-A with the Club Soda. Now he is asking my co-worker:

— So, are you married?

— Is that a wedding band?

— Do you color your hair?

— Where do you stay in Maui?

— How long have you flown?

— Are you always this quiet?

By now she has grabbed a garbage bag and is doing an "aisle check."

Time passes, a few more beverages, a little more ice, a lot more garbage, and a few more questions.

"Ladies and gentlemen, at this time we will be handing out your landing forms to allow you to visit the state of Hawaii." About 89 questions regarding the completion of these forms.

The flight attendant in the back reports that the tray table in 31-F will not stay up and requires a "write up" so that it is repaired in Maui. The passenger in row 4 (remember the tea) says his girlfriend needs an air sick bag, (probably because of the tea)!

The flight attendant "call button" rings in 19-A and the passenger says that her husband feels faint; ok, get his seat tilted back, turn on all air vents, get an oxygen bottle, ask the captain to call the doctor on the ground, obtain information regarding the passenger. Have one flight attendant stay with row 19.

The passenger in row 4 calls to ask for another air sick bag.

Passenger in 22-A rings the flight attendant "call button" to say that her reading light does not work!

At this time the flight attendants will be passing through the cabin with another beverage service. Along with this service we will be serving you a choice of pretzels or a cookie. You know how this will go . . . row 1 all want pretzels, row 2 all want cookies, row 3 wants both pretzels and cookies and we have 28 more rows to go! "Unfortunately" we only carry enough for one or the other. We will get back to you if there are any left! We have 3 pretzels and 2 cookies left!

"Ladies and gentlemen, the seat belt sign will be illuminated in just a few minutes indicating our decent into Maui. Please take this time to use the restroom or run any errands that you may have prior to landing."

"The captain has turned on the seat belt sign. Please turn off and stow all electronic devices and restow all of your carry on items. Fasten your seat belts and remain seated for the duration of this flight."

Final decent into Maui—"Please return all seatbacks and tray tables to their upright and locked position. The cabin lights will be turned off for landing. We will be on the ground shortly."

Here go the flight attendant call lights:

19-A—Will a doctor meet my husband on the aircraft?

7-A—Do you need my landing form?

17-B—Can I keep this can of beer to take with me?

14-C—Can I give you this napkin?

4-C—My mother is waiting for me. Can I get off first?

"Ladies and gentlemen, on behalf of this airline and this entire flight crew, welcome to Maui.

Federal regulations require that you remain seated until the aircraft comes to a complete stop at the gate and the seat belt sign has been turned off. It has been our pleasure serving most of you!"

Aloha and enjoy Maui.